SOMATIC THERAPY FOR TRAUMA

QUICK EXERCISES TO RELEASE EMOTIONAL PAIN, AND REGULATE THE NERVOUS SYSTEM FOR A POWERFUL MIND-BODY CONNECTION, HEIGHTENED INTUITION AND INNER PEACE

JOY DEVEREAUX

Disclaimer Notice:

Please note the information contained within this document is for educational and entertainment purposes only. All effort has been expended to present accurate, up-to-date, and reliable, complete information. No warranties of any kind are declared or implied. Readers acknowledge that the author is not engaging in the rendering of legal, financial, medical or professional advice. The content within this book has been derived from various sources. Please consult a licensed professional before attempting any techniques outlined in this book.

By reading this document, the reader agrees that under no circumstances is the author responsible for any losses, direct or indirect, which are incurred as a result of the use of the information contained within this document, including, but not limited to, — errors, omissions, or inaccuracies.

Medical Disclaimer Notice:

The information provided in this book is for educational and informational purposes only and is not intended as medical advice. Somatic therapy techniques and practices described herein may not be suitable for everyone. Always consult with a qualified healthcare professional or mental health provider before starting any new therapeutic approach, especially if you have a history of trauma, mental health issues, or medical conditions. This book does not substitute for professional care, and the author is not responsible for any outcomes resulting from the use of the techniques or information presented.

Dedication

*To my boys, Big G and Little G. You are my heart outside my body.
The catalyst for my growth, the reason I strive to be a better person
every day, and why I seek to heal my wounds so you won't have to heal
from me. Thank you for being the amazing humans you are and the joy
you bring to my life.*

With all my love, Mom

*To my husband, Matt, for all your support and for being my rock when
I feel untethered. I'm confident I would not be who I am today without
having you in my corner all these years. I love you.*

Love, Me

CONTENTS

INTRODUCTION

There I was perched on the blue velvet chair, sunlight pouring in through the window of the therapist's waiting room. I was casually flipping through a new Ted Lasso quote book that was sitting on the side table, its lighthearted wisdom a welcome distraction. This had been my Thursday ritual for the last year—dropping off the kids, squeezing in errands, then plopping into this chair to prepare for another round of recounting my life's dramas.

I had seen my fair share of professionals at different points in my life who simply nodded and said, "That sounds tough." I needed more than just being told my feelings were valid. Not to mention, I felt like a broken record, having to retell my back story over and over again. Finding an engaging and trustworthy therapist felt so laborious and, at times, downright hopeless, quite honestly. But my new therapist was different. She listened with genuine curiosity and empathy, and it felt great to sense progress finally. I had some "breakthroughs and aha moments, yet after several months of talk therapy, I found myself circling back to the same old themes, sharing similar stories that echoed familiar pain. It dawned on me that no matter how much I shared, it seemed impossible to fully release everything weighing me down. Therapy had helped me reframe my thoughts, but that nagging feeling of being "stuck" still lingered.

After sharing my feelings with my therapist, she suggested a technique that uses bilateral stimulation to aid in the processing of traumatic memories. She passed me two small handheld paddles that alternately buzzed in each hand, and I braced myself for what I assumed would be a mildly unsettling but manageable exercise. The memory that popped into my head seemed relatively innocuous compared to the plethora of others on my "trauma timeline." Yet, I started to relive the memory as if I was transported back in time. I was seven years old again, being shoved up the stairs by the brother of my Mom's new boyfriend, who I had never met until two hours ago. He's mad, yelling at me and accusing me of stealing from the general store we had just visited to get some candy, while my Mom's voice echoes from downstairs, "You better not have!" Of course, I didn't! I never stole anything, and she knew that! How could she say that?! As I held those paddles, my emotions roared to life; I was experiencing that chaotic, icy fear and indignation all over again. Cue the emotional floodgates. My skin felt cold and clammy; my heart was pounding, my chest felt tight, and my brain was racing with different scenarios of how I would kick this guy hard, right where it counted if I needed to. Then came the sadness and helplessness over the realization that my Mom was not coming to save me or even help me! She is my mother; why is she not protecting me? Can't she hear the fear in my voice, my pleas for help, and the adamance in my tone that "I did not do it!" - Did that even matter? My eyes started to sting, and the hot tears came like a leaky faucet, slowly at first, then quickly turning into a steady stream. My body felt tight and full of prickly energy and rage- oh, the rage, fury, and even loathing that stemmed from such severe disappointment. It had all been uprooted, and it felt like it was happening to me in that moment all over again, but it wasn't. I was safely sitting at the end of my therapist's stiff, aqua-colored tweed sofa. We finished the exercise. Whew! She handed me a tissue and guided me through a grounding exercise called rooting to bring me back to the present moment and some deep-paced breathing to steady my nervous system. This was to remind and reassure my body that I was a safe, full-grown adult, not a seven-year-old in distress. It was incredible how the simple somatic exercises helped soothe me and restore my sense of stability after that ordeal. To top it off, as I recount this experience to you, I notice that I'm not reliving it. It feels familiar but distant, like watching an action movie at home on TV versus in an IMAX theater in 3D with surround sound. The intensity is real, but the sensation is oddly muted. That's the power of somatic therapy: it allows you to experience, process, and eventually distance yourself from those overwhelming emotions, making them less of a daily burden and more of a past story you can finally let go of. This concept reminds me of a quote from *As Good as True* by Cheryl Reid; she says, "That feeling you have, how sad you are about your mama, won't ever go away," she said. "It's not supposed to. But one day, it'll be like those trees over there, not like these here."

Usually, when I felt overwhelmed, I would try to be stronger and suppress my emotions by pushing them away or just waiting for them to fade. I never realized I had the option—or the power—to simply allow those feelings to be there, acknowledge them, truly feel them, and use my breath and senses to let them pass naturally and bring me back to reality. My world opened up that day and I started to realize my ability to expand my capacity to handle big emotions and find ease inside myself. This introduction opened my eyes to a different approach to accessing and processing trauma—one that emphasizes feeling it rather than just talking or thinking through it. If you are someone who feels like you have tried everything- talk therapy, medication, meditation—but nothing seems to ease the constant tension and unsettling feeling in your body, as if your trauma has you locked in a cage. Then, allow somatic therapy to be the key that sets you free.

When you experience trauma, there's a tendency to get stuck in your head, which rarely leads to the solutions you want or need. Instead of trying to think your way out of a situation, it's more useful to take action and shift your mindset. If you find that your typical reactions to the effects of trauma are problematic, then somatic therapy offers a great opportunity to explore this with curiosity. Your trauma has crafted a story that may hold you back, but what if you could rewrite that narrative? Imagine choosing a new story that empowers you. Doesn't that feel freeing?

By reading this book, you can expect to gain both a conceptual knowledge of somatic therapy and practical skills. This isn't just a theoretical guide; it's designed for you to take action. We will begin by exploring the basics of somatic therapy, helping you understand what it is, how it works, and why it's effective for addressing trauma. Next, we'll delve into the nature of trauma itself, discussing how it affects the body and mind for a better understanding of the real consequences of your trauma on multiple levels. This establishes the foundation for enhancing your emotional well-being. You might have some curiosity or skepticism about somatic therapy, which is completely normal. Many people wonder if it will work for them or if it's based on solid science. So this book dives into the fascinating neuroscience behind it, uncovering the "why" and "how, and shares inspiring success stories demonstrating its power, transforming doubt into hope. You'll also find more details on tailoring somatic therapy to different types of trauma and how to combine somatic therapy with other therapeutic approaches, ensuring that you find practices that resonate with your unique experiences. You'll discover how crucial body awareness is and learn simple techniques for embodiment that you can easily incorporate into your everyday life, guiding you through creating your own daily practice. For busy schedules, we'll also cover micro-practices that fit seamlessly into your existing routine, allowing you to engage in somatic practices even on hectic days. I encourage you to engage actively with the content. Try the exercises, reflect on your experiences, and use what makes the most sense for you. Finally, we'll focus on celebrating your progress, no matter how small, as you build your repertoire for release and healing. By the end, you'll feel empowered with practical strategies and tools to apply what you learn to your daily life to release tension and emotional pain, alleviate stress, and regulate your nervous system for a powerful mind-body connection, heightened intuition, and inner peace.

Healing is possible. Rest assured that everything you need to heal is already inside you. Our bodies have so much wisdom to share when we listen. Somatic therapy helps you connect the dots, giving you clarity and insight into your experiences. You have the strength within you to overcome trauma and lead a fulfilling life. So, take a deep breath, embrace this moment, and let this be the beginning of your own transformative adventure.

THE BASICS OF SOMATIC THERAPY

"Go from a participant to a protagonist in your own story."

- JIM KWIK

I f you've ever felt disconnected from your body or your emotions are too overwhelming to handle, this approach could offer the relief you've been seeking. It's particularly beneficial for those who feel that traditional talk therapy hasn't fully addressed their needs. Rather than discussing traumatic experiences in detail, somatic therapy focuses on the connection between the mind and body, encouraging you to explore physical sensations and emotions. This can create a gentler way to healing, allowing for gradual awareness and processing of trauma. Remember, somatic therapy isn't about replacing other therapies but complementing them. It adds another tool to your healing toolbox.

WHAT IS SOMATIC THERAPY?

In somatic therapy, the body takes center stage in healing. Derived from the Greek word "soma," meaning body, this holistic approach recognizes that trauma isn't just a mental memory—it's a physical experience etched into our cells, muscles, tissues, and nerves. Unlike traditional talk therapies that focus on thoughts and emotions, somatic therapy tunes into the body's silent language. Picture your body as a living archive, a vessel of every emotional trauma you've endured. These unresolved experiences can manifest as everything from nagging tension and discomfort to debilitating pain, creating a heavy backlog of stress that burdens the body.

Somatic therapy aims to help you become a skilled interpreter of your body's signals by using techniques like movement, mindfulness, breathwork, and gentle touch to help you reconnect with your body and release the trapped emotions. By developing this awareness, you can process and release trauma in ways that talking alone often can't achieve. It's like harmonizing the entire symphony instead of adjusting just one string. By addressing the whole person—body, mind, and spirit—somatic therapy offers a gateway to profound transformation.

Somatic therapy serves as a powerful resource for anyone working through the aftermath of their trauma, inviting you to reconnect with your body and rediscover your strength. This includes individuals with PTSD, complex trauma, emotional trauma, physical or sexual trauma, and relationship trauma. If you've ever felt like your body is carrying the weight of your past, somatic therapy might be for you. It's also advantageous for those dealing with chronic pain and tension, anxiety, grief, trust and intimacy issues, self-esteem problems, and developmental and attachment challenges. Imagine you've been carrying a heavy backpack for years. Over time, you get used to the weight, but it still slows you down and causes pain. Somatic therapy helps you unpack that backpack, one item at a time, making it lighter and easier to carry. This process is invaluable not only for trauma recovery but also for seeking self-discovery and personal growth.

Somatic therapy brings a wealth of benefits that can truly change your life, including improved nervous system regulation, which means you're better equipped to deal with stress and emotional triggers—an enhanced mind-body connection, contributing to increased self-awareness and inner peace. Reduced trauma symptoms translate to better sleep, less anxiety, and the ability to enjoy everyday activities without the constant shadow of past events. Increased emotional resilience helps you bounce back from setbacks more quickly, and more self-compassion allows you to treat yourself with the empathy and acceptance you deserve.

Reflection Activity:

So ask yourself . . .

• If you could silence the doubting voices in your head—how much more confidently would you pursue that promotion you've been eyeing, knowing you truly deserve it?

• What if you could stop ruminating over every conversation and feel secure in your relationships—how much deeper would your connections with loved ones become without the weight of overthinking?

• How would it feel to release the old untrue stories your trauma has been telling you that have been holding you back—what new possibilities would open up in your life if you could fully engage in your passions and relationships?

ESSENTIAL PRINCIPLES OF SOMATIC THERAPY

Imagine trying to drive a car without paying attention to the road. Sounds like a recipe for disaster, right? Your body is that car, and your awareness is what keeps it on the road. Trauma often causes us to disconnect from our bodies, making it harder to live life fully. By cultivating body awareness, you begin to recognize the physical sensations accompanying your emotions and experiences. These sensations are like signposts guiding you back to yourself. When you pay attention to your body, you start to understand where it holds tension, where it feels relaxed, and how it responds to different situations.

Presence and mindfulness are the glue that holds somatic therapy together. Staying present means fully engaging in the current moment, not lost in the past or worrying about the future. Mindfulness involves observing your bodily sensations without trying to change them. It's about being a curious observer of your own experience. Think of it as having a front-row seat to your own life. When you practice mindfulness, you create a space to allow things to be as they are, which often leads to clarity and new healthy perspectives. You also become more attuned to your body's needs and signs, making it easier to address them. Small acts of mindfulness anchor you in the present moment, reducing anxiety and helping you feel more secure. When you're present, you're more able to deal with whatever comes your way because you're not distracted by the noise of past traumas or future worries.

Embodiment is a cornerstone of somatic therapy, inviting you to reconnect with your body and experience the present moment fully. It's about tuning into the sensations that arise—whether it's the flutter of anxiety in your stomach or warmth spreading through your limbs. Just as a thermometer measures temperature, embodiment helps you gauge your internal state, allowing you to notice when things feel off-kilter. Instead of ignoring or rushing through these feelings, you embrace them, creating a dialogue between your mind and body. By paying attention to how emotions manifest physically, you begin to understand the stories your body tells and learn to release what no longer serves you. This practice transforms how you engage with yourself, allowing you to cultivate a stronger sense of safety and presence in your own skin. The value of this cannot be understated, as Gabor Maté explains in "The Body Says No," "Safety is a feeling in the body, not a thought in the mind."

Safety and comfort are paramount in somatic therapy. Creating a safe and comfortable environment allows you to explore your emotions and sensations without fear. This might mean setting up a dedicated spot in your home—a corner with soft lighting, comfortable seating, and perhaps some soothing scents like lavender or chamomile essential oil or sounds from a white noise machine (or even binaural beats on your headphones). The goal is to create a sanctuary where you feel secure enough to let your guard down. Trauma often leaves us feeling vulnerable and exposed. By establishing a safe space, you signal to your nervous system that it's okay to relax and let go.

Each principle supports the others, forming a cohesive framework that addresses both the physical and emotional aspects of trauma. By cultivating body awareness, you lay the foundation for more discovery and self-reflection. Presence and mindfulness help you stay engaged in the healing process, while safety and comfort provide the necessary environment for exploration.

THE OBJECTIVES FOR SOMATIC THERAPY AS A HOLISTIC HEALING APPROACH

The first major objective is emotional regulation. Imagine your emotions as a wild river, sometimes gentle and serene, other times raging and uncontrollable. Somatic therapy serves as a skilled river guide, helping you find your way through the treacherous rapids and find smoother waters. By becoming more attuned to your body's signals, you can identify emotional triggers before they sweep you away. In the following chapters, you will learn different exercises to help you stay anchored, even when the emotional currents get rough and turbulent. Over time, you'll find that you can experience your emotions fully without being overwhelmed by them. It's like upgrading from a flimsy raft to a sturdy boat, giving you the stability to ride out the storms.

Another goal is the reduction of trauma symptoms such as anxiety, stress, and emotional dysregulation. When trauma is weighing you down in both mind and body, somatic therapy aims to lighten this load by addressing the root causes of your symptoms. For instance, anxiety often manifests as a tight chest or a racing heart. By tuning into these sensory experiences, you can use somatic techniques to release the tension. Stress, on the other hand, might show up as chronic pain or digestive issues. Somatic therapy teaches you to listen to these signals and respond with empathy rather than frustration. Over time, you'll notice that the intensity and frequency of these symptoms diminish, just as an adversary loses their power when you stop engaging in the conflict.

When it comes to flashbacks and intrusive memories, it can feel like a relentless loop of past horrors. Somatic therapy helps break this cycle by processing and releasing the trauma stored in your body by allowing you to revisit traumatic memories in a controlled, manageable way. This gradual exposure helps desensitize your nervous system, reducing the power these memories hold over you. It's similar to turning the volume down on a blaring radio, allowing you to finally hear your own thoughts again. The result is a calmer mind, a more relaxed body, and the freedom to live in the present rather than be trapped in the past.

Another key objective is to improve the mind-body connection. Before you say, "We've already covered that," it's important to note that the distinction lies in the fact that while body awareness and the mind-body connection represent the desired outcome of therapy, they also serve as the way to achieve that outcome. In our fast-paced, technology-driven world, it's easy to become disconnected from our bodies. We spend hours hunched over screens, ignoring our bodies' signals until they scream for attention. Somatic therapy helps you rebuild this vital connection by encouraging you to tune into what your body already knows but your brain may not. You gain insight into your patterns and behaviors by exploring the physical sensations and emotions stored in your body. You might uncover deep-seated beliefs or unresolved emotions driving your actions. This self-discovery process can be both challenging and liberating, offering you the opportunity to heal old wounds and make conscious choices moving forward. You'll find that by enhancing the mind-body connection, you'll have a magnified sense of harmony within yourself, making it easier to manage life's ups and downs.

Somatic therapy also emphasizes the importance of self-nurturing and non-judgment. Trauma often leaves us with a harsh inner critic, constantly judging and berating ourselves. Somatic practices encourage you to treat yourself with kindness and understanding. By checking in with your body's signals, you learn to respond with supportiveness rather than criticism. This allows you to release old patterns and embrace new possibilities. You'll find that you have more patience with yourself and others, creating a ripple effect of positive change in your life.

Unlike approaches focusing solely on the mind or body, somatic therapy recognizes that true healing involves both. It's like tending to a garden: you can't just water the plants and ignore the soil; you must nurture both to see growth. This holistic approach integrates various techniques to address the physical, emotional, and psychological aspects and multifaceted nature of trauma. These techniques help steady the nervous system, release stored tension, and provide a sense of safety and stability so you can feel at home in your own body.

The therapeutic objectives of somatic therapy extend beyond symptom relief; they aim for true self-improvement and lasting change - changes that transform many aspects of your life. As you become more attuned to your body and emotions, you'll develop a higher sense of self-awareness and resilience. You'll learn to trust your body's signals and respond with empathy rather than judgment. This self-awareness builds a stronger connection with yourself and others, enhancing your relationships and overall quality of life. You'll find that you have more energy, greater emotional stability, and a renewed sense of purpose.

THE PROFOUND IMPACT OF TRAUMA

" I can be changed by what happens to me, but I refuse to be reduced by it."

- MAYA ANGELOU

Trauma has a way of changing us, often in ways that are invisible to others but deeply felt by us. If you've ever felt like you've lost a piece of yourself after a traumatic event, you're not alone. Trauma can leave an indelible mark on both your body and mind. This chapter is focused on the fundamental characteristics and effects of trauma as well as how it is experienced, processed, and expressed. We will also examine the role of your nervous system and the reactions you may experience after trauma.

THE NATURE OF TRAUMA

Trauma isn't just an emotional hiccup; it's more like a complicated dance between your brain and body that can feel a bit like a chaotic flash mob. When you experience trauma, your brain and body go into survival mode. This can involve a flood of stress hormones like cortisol and adrenaline, which prepare you to either fight, flight/flee, or freeze, which you may have learned about in a psychology class back in high school or college. You may be left in a constant state of alertness or feeling perpetually stuck, unable to move forward or fully engage with the world around you. These reactions are incredibly useful in the moment but can become problematic or even debilitating if they persist long after the threat has passed. Peter Levine, the creator of Somatic Experiencing®, emphasizes, "Trauma is not just an event that took place sometime in the past; it is also the imprint that the event leaves on the mind, brain, and body."

Let's break down the different types of trauma, starting with acute trauma, which is like a surprise thunderstorm that leaves you soaked but is over in a flash. Acute trauma results from a single, isolated incident, like an accident, assault, or natural disaster. Imagine it as a sudden, violent storm that wreaks havoc but eventually passes. Chronic trauma, on the other hand, is like living in a never-ending storm. It involves repeated and prolonged exposure to stressors, such as ongoing abuse or living in a war zone. Complex trauma is a tangled web of multiple traumatic events, often invasive and interpersonal in nature, occurring over an extended period. Similarly, collective trauma affects entire communities, manifesting in shared emotional wounds from events like wars or natural disasters, and can encompass racial trauma, where systemic oppression and violence impact the well-being of marginalized groups. Intergenerational trauma highlights how the effects of trauma can ripple through families, impacting future generations who have not directly experienced the initial events.

Trauma comes in various flavors, each with its own unique implications. Similar to how boiling water affects an egg and a potato differently, trauma shapes us differently. Physical trauma involves actual injuries, like broken bones, severe wounds, or bruises, while emotional trauma often stems from experiences like betrayal or loss. These emotional scars can be sneaky; their invisibility makes them easier to ignore, adding to the distress. Such psychological trauma messes with your mental state, sometimes leading to conditions like PTSD, anxiety, or depression. And don't forget secondary trauma—when you are indirectly exposed to trauma, such as through supporting a loved one through a traumatic event. Think of it as trauma by proxy; it can be just as heavy as direct trauma, leading to feelings of helplessness and emotional exhaustion.

In the immediate aftermath, trauma can leave you feeling shocked and numb, as if your brain has pressed "pause" to shield you from reality. While this can serve as a temporary coping mechanism, it often results in a sense of disconnection from yourself and others, presenting as a feeling of dissociation and apathy. Over time, those initial feelings might evolve into long-term anxiety or chronic stress, making everyday life feel like an uphill battle- where it is hard to relax or feel safe. You might find yourself constantly on edge, waiting for the next disaster to strike. These long-term repercussions can intertwine with every aspect of your life, from your relationships to your ability to work or enjoy leisure activities.

Cultural perspectives on trauma also play a significant role. In some societies, trauma may carry a stigma, leading people to feel ashamed or reluctant to seek help because it is seen as a sign of weakness or a personal failing. In others, a communal approach fosters sharing burdens and community healing, recognizing trauma as a collective experience. Acknowledging cultural intricacies opens more doors to recovery and healing.

The stigma surrounding trauma can be a serious barrier to recovery. Many people feel pressure to "just get over it," which overlooks the reality that trauma requires compassion, understanding, and sometimes professional support. This is often reinforced by societal attitudes that prioritize stoicism and self-reliance. Trauma is not something you can simply will away. Challenging these beliefs helps to create a more supportive environment for everyone.

By recognizing the different forms of trauma and their immediate and long-term effects, you can begin to see the complete picture of how it has shaped you. And by exploring cultural and societal perspectives, you can find the support and validation you need to start healing. Remember, trauma is not a life sentence. With the right tools and support, you can move towards a future filled with hope and resilience.

HOW TRAUMA MANIFESTS IN THE BODY

When trauma goes unaddressed, it can really turn your body into a bit of a troublemaker. You might find yourself dealing with physical symptoms that don't have any clear medical explanation but are linked to emotional distress. Suddenly, you're experiencing aches and pains that seem to come out of nowhere, as if your body is trying to tell you something important. These physical manifestations are your body's way of saying, "Hey, something's not right!" much like the check engine light on your dashboard.

. . .

For example, fibromyalgia, often characterized by widespread pain and tenderness, is frequently linked to unresolved trauma. Your muscles might feel perpetually tight like you're always bracing for impact. That tension can lead to unexplained stiffness, making it tough to move around comfortably. This is why chronic physical symptoms—remnants of trauma—often persist long after the initial event. When your body's defenses are perpetually on high alert, it is draining on your energy and resources. Functional neurological symptom disorder is another example, where trauma leads to neurological symptoms like seizures or paralysis without a clear medical explanation. These symptoms can be incredibly frustrating, making you feel like your body is betraying you.

Your digestive system can also take a hit, leading to issues like irritable bowel syndrome (IBS) and acid reflux. In fact, an article in the American College of Physicians found that 44% of women seeking treatment for severe GI disturbances reported a history of abuse, highlighting the deep connection between trauma and digestive health. You might experience frequent stomachaches, bloating, or other "tummy troubles." Ever had a "gut-wrenching" experience? That's not just a figure of speech. Or maybe you've felt like your stomach was" tied in knots." This discomfort may hinder your ability to enjoy meals and maintain healthy eating habits, often leading to skipped meals or choosing less nutritious options. On top of that, chronic stress can weaken your immune system, leaving you feeling more vulnerable to infections or getting sick. All that elderberry syrup, echinacea, and bee propolis will only get you so far when your body is constantly in a state of stress.

. . .

One of the more intriguing and perplexing aspects of trauma is how it can be stored in the body as a somatic memory. Your body can store traumatic experiences as physical sensations and memories. Your body keeps track of past experiences, and when something triggers those memories, it can feel like the trauma is happening all over again. It's as if your body has a hidden library of past events, with each trauma tucked away in its own little compartment. When something triggers these memories, your body reacts as if the trauma is happening all over again. The biological processes involved in storing trauma in the body are complex. Trauma can reshape the way your brain processes and stores memories, leading to changes in your nervous system and hormone levels. This can lead to physical sensations like tension, rapid heartbeat, or shortness of breath. You might find yourself breaking out in a cold sweat, feeling a knot in your stomach, or experiencing unexplained pain in specific areas of your body. Some people report feeling a tingling sensation in their limbs or a sense of heaviness in their chest. Others might suddenly feel dizzy or nauseous or experience a dry mouth and trembling hands. These physical reactions can occur seemingly out of nowhere, triggered by a sight, sound, smell, or even a particular body position that reminds your system of the traumatic event, even if you're not consciously aware of the connection.

As you can see, trauma is far-reaching. You might find it difficult to concentrate, as your mind is constantly preoccupied with intrusive thoughts or memories. Trauma can affect your work, relationships, and overall quality of life. Fatigue and sleep disturbances are also common. You might struggle with insomnia, nightmares, or restless sleep, leaving you feeling exhausted and drained. So, trauma is much more than just an emotional experience; it's a full-body affair that bleeds into many aspects of your life. Recognizing how it manifests in the body allows you to address these symptoms and work towards a more balanced state of well-being.

THE MIND-BODY CONNECTION IN TRAUMA

Have you ever noticed how your entire body tenses up when you're stressed? That's not just in your head—it's your body reacting to your emotions. The interconnectedness of your mind and body is a fundamental aspect of how you experience trauma and its aftermath. We will frequently refer to this connection throughout this book because it is foundational to somatic therapy. The influence between your physical health and mental well-being is a two-way street. While your mind affects your body, your body also has the power to influence your mind. This can be used to your advantage. When your mind has, well, "a mind of its own," you can use your body to engage the body to get the brain to release endorphins, those feel-good chemicals that boost your mood and reduce stress.

Understanding the mind-body connection as it relates to trauma also means recognizing the power of small, consistent actions. You don't have to make drastic changes overnight. Simple somatic practices can have a cumulative effect on your well-being. Once again, it involves creating a dialogue between your mind and body, listening to what each has to say, and responding with kindness.

So, the next time you feel a knot in your stomach or a tightness in your chest, take a moment to pause and listen. What is your body trying to tell you? Paying attention to these signals and addressing them with somatic practices can create a more harmonious relationship between your mind and body.

THE ROLE OF THE NERVOUS SYSTEM IN TRAUMA

Your nervous system acts as the command center of your body, orchestrating everything from your heartbeat to your emotional responses. When trauma strikes, this command center can go haywire. The autonomic nervous system (ANS) plays a critical role here, and it's divided into two main parts: the sympathetic (which prepares you for action) and parasympathetic (which settles you down) nervous systems. Consider the sympathetic nervous system, your body's gas pedal. When activated, it prepares you to face danger by flooding your system with adrenaline and cortisol. Your heart rate spikes, your pupils dilate, and your muscles tense, ready for action. This is great if a lion is chasing you, but not so much if you're simply reliving a traumatic memory while you're driving down the street.

Conversely, the parasympathetic nervous system acts as your body's brake pedal. It slows your heart rate, promoting digestion and relaxation after the threat has passed. Ideally, these two systems work in harmony, balancing each other out. But trauma can throw this off, causing your sympathetic nervous system to stay stuck in overdrive. This constant state of alertness can be exhausting and debilitating, making it hard to relax or feel safe. Dysregulation affects not only physical symptoms but also neurotransmitter levels in your brain. For instance, chronic activation of the sympathetic nervous system can lower serotonin levels, leading to mood disorders, while disrupting dopamine pathways can sway motivation and pleasure. This is why balancing these systems is so critical.

To take this a step further, let's talk about Polyvagal Theory, introduced by Dr. Stephen Porges. This theory highlights the vagus nerve, which plays a vital role in managing how our bodies respond to stress. Your vagal tone—the health of your vagus nerve—can considerably determine your emotional resilience. When you have a high vagal tone, you're better equipped to handle stress, recover quickly, and maintain a sense of steadiness. On the other hand, a low vagal tone can leave you feeling overwhelmed and more reactive, making it harder to manage emotional ups and downs and bounce back from challenges. You can even track your vagal tone using a heart rate variability (HRV) monitor, which measures the variations in time between your heartbeats. A healthy heart rate variability (HRV) range typically falls between 60 to 100 milliseconds for most people. Higher HRV values are generally associated with a well-functioning autonomic nervous system and better stress resilience, while lower HRV may indicate stress or imbalance. However, that is more a guideline than a rule. Keep in mind that optimal HRV can vary based on individual factors, including age, fitness level, and overall health.

The vagus nerve is instrumental in shaping social interactions, aiding in connections with others, and nurturing feelings of safety and trust. When the vagus nerve functions well, you're more skilled at managing social interactions and building meaningful relationships. This connection to the social engagement system underscores the importance of addressing trauma not only on an individual level but also within the context of your community and relationships.

Navigating the aftermath of trauma can be incredibly challenging, especially when your nervous system is thrown into a state of chaos. Trauma often leads to dysregulation, creating a chaotic internal environment characterized by hyperarousal and hypoarousal. In a state of hyperarousal, you might feel perpetually on edge—jumpy, irritable, and struggling to focus. Even a loud noise or unexpected movement can trigger a wave of panic. On the other hand, hypoarousal can leave you feeling numb, disconnected, or lethargic, as if your body has pressed the "pause" button to shield you from emotional overload. If you are thinking this sounds awfully similar to the "freeze" state, you're right! Though Hypoarousal and the freeze state are closely related, they are not identical; they are more like fraternal twins. Hypoarousal is when your body and emotions become less active, causing feelings of numbness or tiredness. The freeze state is a specific reaction where you feel stuck or unable to move due to trauma or intense stress. Essentially, all freeze states involve hypoarousal, but not all hypoarousal experiences are freeze responses. Similar to the concept that a square can be a rectangle (by definition), but a rectangle cannot be a square. So many nuances here-right?

The implications of a dysregulated nervous system are far-reaching. You might find it challenging to maintain relationships, perform well at work, or even take care of yourself. Your quality of life can suffer greatly as you grapple with these intense physical and emotional reactions.

In addressing trauma and its influence on your nervous system, the goal is to expand your "window of tolerance," a concept that refers to the range of arousal levels within which you can function optimally. When your nervous system is regulated, you feel more stable and resilient and have the ability to deal with stress and emotional triggers. It's like increasing the bandwidth of your emotional internet connection, allowing you to process experiences without becoming overwhelmed. By recognizing how trauma reconfigures your sympathetic and parasympathetic responses and by leveraging concepts like polyvagal theory, you can better manage your stress and build emotional resilience.

COMMON TRAUMA RESPONSES AND THEIR SOMATIC SIGNS

Trauma can embed itself deeply, affecting your emotions, behaviors, and physical health. One of the most common emotional responses to trauma is anxiety. You might find your heart racing, palms sweating, or chest tightening at seemingly random moments. Panic attacks can swoop in like uninvited guests, leaving you gasping for air and feeling like you're losing control. Depression often follows close behind, casting a shadow over your days with a persistent feeling of despair. It's not just about feeling sad; it's more like a heavy fog that numbs your emotions and saps your energy.

On top of emotional responses, there are also behavioral reactions, such as avoidance behaviors. You might find yourself steering clear of places, people, or situations that remind you of a traumatic event. This can be isolating as you build walls to protect yourself from potential triggers. Hypervigilance is another common reaction. It's like having a radar that's constantly scanning for danger. This, too, can lead you to feel on edge, jumpy, or easily startled. This heightened state of alertness can be exhausting, once again making it difficult to relax or feel safe. Hypervigilance can also lead to sleep disturbances, further exacerbating the emotional toll of trauma.

Trauma can also lead to irrational behaviors, often as a misguided attempt to cope with overwhelming emotions and sensations. When the brain's stress response is activated, it can distort your perception of reality, making situations seem more threatening than they actually are. This can result in impulsive decisions, aggressive outbursts, or self-destructive actions. For example, someone might lash out at loved ones or engage in risky behaviors, driven by the fight-or-flight response that is stuck in overdrive. These reactions can feel confusing and disorienting as they don't align with your true values or intentions. They are just your body's way of alerting you to unresolved trauma. Understanding the source of these behaviors gives you the ability to have compassion for yourself. By recognizing and addressing these markers, you can begin to unravel the clutch of trauma for healthier behavior moving forward.

Your body doesn't stay silent in the face of trauma, either. There's a long list of undesirable physical responses that we discussed earlier, from pain in various parts of your body to a range of gut issues. It's not just in your head—your body is reacting to the stress and anxiety. Identifying these responses is once again an opportunity to check in with your body. Are you clenching your jaw? Are your shoulders hunched up to your ears? Simply noticing these physical reactions can help you start to release them.

THE SCIENCE BEHIND SOMATIC HEALING AND WHY IT IS EFFECTIVE

"Courage doesn't happen when you have all the answers. It happens when you are ready to face all the questions you have avoided your whole life"

- SHANNON ADLER

Somatic therapy revolutionizes trauma healing by leveraging the interplay between body and mind. This connection can manifest in surprising ways. For instance, you may find yourself doing something completely inane, like making a cup of tea, yet your body suddenly reacts as if you're in immediate danger. This bewildering experience is a hallmark of how trauma can hijack your brain and body, making everyday moments feel like life-and-death situations. To understand why this happens, we'll need to delve into the fascinating and complex world of neuroscience, shedding light on how our brains and bodies respond to adverse experiences. Then, we'll examine the unique elements that make somatic therapy particularly powerful for many so many people, highlighting real-life examples through compelling case studies and personal stories that demonstrate the life-changing outcomes of this therapeutic method.

THE NEUROSCIENCE OF TRAUMA AND HEALING

When trauma strikes, it dramatically transforms several key regions of your brain, altering both its structure and chemistry. One significant change is the imbalance of cortisol and adrenaline, the primary stress hormones. The amygdala, often referred to as the brain's alarm system, is responsible for detecting threats and triggering the fight-or-flight response we covered earlier. When you experience trauma, this almond-shaped cluster of neurons goes full throttle, releasing large amounts of these hormones, making you hyper-alert to potential dangers and preparing you for immediate action. Imagine a smoke detector that triggers not only at the sight of smoke or fire but also from the slightest bit of steam from boiling water. This heightened state of alertness can be overwhelming and exhausting, making it difficult to relax or feel safe. The chronic stress of this can lead to an overproduction of cortisol, which can have several detrimental ramifications on your health, such as a suppression of your immune system, increased blood pressure, and even damage to your brain over time.

Somatic therapy helps to rebalance these neurochemical levels. By doing so, your parasympathetic nervous system gets activated, which counteracts the effects of cortisol and adrenaline. Furthermore, this activation prompts the release of endorphins, your body's natural painkillers and mood elevators. Endorphins not only reduce pain but also induce feelings of pleasure and well-being. It's like your brain's way of giving you a little high-five for taking care of yourself.

. . .

The brain's memory center is also affected. The hippocampus is the part of the brain responsible for forming and retrieving memories. However, when you experience trauma, this seahorse-shaped structure can become impaired. Studies have shown that traumatic stress can reduce the volume of the hippocampus, affecting your ability to process and store new memories. This shrinkage can also contribute to the fragmented, disjointed memories often associated with PTSD. Imagine trying to piece together a puzzle with missing pieces—it's frustrating and hard to see the big picture.

Additionally, trauma can substantially impair the prefrontal cortex, the brain's executive control center responsible for decision-making, emotional regulation, and impulse control. Any dysfunction reduces its ability to keep the amygdala in check. It's like a circus without a ring leader —utter chaos. Without the prefrontal cortex's subduing influence, the amygdala runs rampant, causing heightened anxiety and emotional dysregulation. This dysfunction can lead to difficulties in concentrating, making decisions, and managing emotions.

The great news is your brain is incredibly resilient, thanks to a phenomenon known as neuroplasticity. Neuroplasticity is the brain's ability to reorganize itself by forming new neural connections. The brain can rewire itself! This adaptive capability allows the brain to recover from trauma and create healthier pathways. Just as a hiker might find a new route when a familiar trail is blocked, your brain can build a new route to get you where you want to go.

Neuroplasticity means that you can reshape your neural pathways through regular practice, creating new, healthier neural connections that can replace the old ones shaped by trauma. For example, if you've always associated a particular smell with a traumatic event, somatic therapy can help you form new associations. Your brain learns to associate it with a sense of safety rather than danger by practicing certain somatic techniques while exposed to that smell. Over time, this process of gradual desensitization reduces the power of the traumatic trigger.

A leading expert in this area of neuroscience is Dr. Joe Dispenza, who has extensively discussed the concept of neuroplasticity in his work. He emphasizes the importance of consistent practice and how it enables us to break free from old habits, patterns, and behaviors. Remember the first time you got a new phone, especially if you switched from an old analog flip phone to a digital smartphone? Initially, your fingers had to get used to swiping and tapping a touch screen instead of pressing buttons, but with regular practice, you got better. The same principle applies to neuroplasticity. The more you practice somatic techniques, the more your brain rewires itself, leading to lasting changes in how you respond to stress and trauma. This reinforces the fact that all you need to heal is already within you.

WHY SOMATIC THERAPY IS EFFECTIVE

The effectiveness of somatic therapy lies in its biological foundation. It actively influences neurotransmitters and brings about measurable changes in both the body and brain by engaging these various change mechanisms to positively alter brain function to promote healing and emotional resilience.

As previously explained, somatic therapy taps directly into your body's innate healing capabilities. It precisely targets the nervous system regulation that trauma often disrupts. Stabilizing these fluctuations guides you back to a more even-keeled state. Somatic therapy is advantageous in two primary ways: It addresses the negative consequences of trauma by helping restore homeostasis to the nervous system and promotes positive healing by engaging the body's natural feel-good chemicals. It lowers stress hormones like cortisol while boosting neurotransmitters such as serotonin and dopamine, enhancing emotional well-being and encouraging physical relief through the release of endorphins. One of the most compelling advantages of somatic therapy is its ability to create those new, healthier neural pathways mentioned previously. Trauma can create deeply ingrained patterns of fear and avoidance. Somatic practices help you break these patterns by forming new associations. Though we've touched on many of these points before, they are also the very reasons why somatic therapy is so effective in fostering healing and stability.

The beauty of somatic therapy's body-based approach lies in its holistic nature, making it a comprehensive solution for healing. By addressing both the physical and emotional aspects of trauma, this method ensures that all facets of your experience are considered. When you engage with your body, you're not just processing emotions but also releasing physical tension and stress that often accompany those feelings. This interconnectedness allows for a deeper level of healing, as it recognizes that emotional wounds can manifest physically and vice versa. This process enables you to reconnect with yourself in a manner that feels both safe and empowering. It's like coming home to your own body, learning to trust it again, and letting it guide you toward healing in a more integrated and cohesive way.

Moreover, somatic practices offer practical, actionable steps to incorporate into your daily life for immediate relief while promoting long-term progress. These techniques are accessible and easy to integrate. As you will see in the next chapter, the simplicity and effectiveness of these practices make them a valuable addition to any trauma recovery approach.

Lastly, Scientific research supports these claims. The findings underscore the efficacy of somatic therapy in addressing the neurochemical imbalances caused by trauma, offering a hopeful perspective on healing. This evidence not only highlights the efficacy of somatic approaches but also empowers you to believe in your ability to heal. Knowing that there are valid options like somatic therapy available can be incredibly encouraging, reminding you that you're not alone in this experience and that positive change is within reach. Embracing these therapies leads you one step closer to discovering your true self, feeling whole, and finding peace.

EVIDENCE OF TRANSFORMATION AND HEALING THROUGH SOMATIC THERAPY

Somatic therapy isn't just a new-age trend; it's backed by a growing body of scientific evidence that highlights its value in treating various forms of trauma. Studies on Somatic Experiencing®, a popular form of somatic therapy, have shown considerable reductions in PTSD symptoms, including anxiety and depression. Another study found that participants who engaged in Somatic Experiencing® reported lower levels of cortisol and higher levels of serotonin and dopamine, indicating improved stress regulation and mood. In another study, K. W. Brown et al. researched the effects of mindfulness and somatic practices on cortisol levels and neurotransmitter balance. The results also indicated that participants engaging in somatic therapy showed notable reductions in cortisol and increases in serotonin and dopamine levels, which correlate with improvements in mood and anxiety.

Further neuroimaging evidence using functional magnetic resonance imaging (fMRI) revealed alterations in brain activity and connectivity after engaging in somatic therapy interventions, indicating that somatic therapy can lead to highly beneficial changes in brain function and structure, particularly in areas associated with emotional regulation and stress response. Additional research on Somatic Experiencing® (SE™), as highlighted in a study published in *Frontiers in Neuroscience*, assessed various parameters related to participants' mental and physical health before and after the intervention. Researchers measured changes in anxiety levels, quality of life, and physical symptoms using standardized scales to ensure accuracy. The results showed an increase in quality of life and a significant decrease in physical symptoms and anxiety, illustrating just how transformative it can be for trauma recovery. (*See following graphs.*)

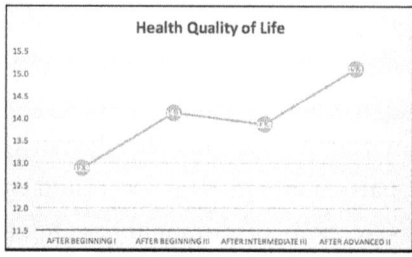

Increased Quality of Life

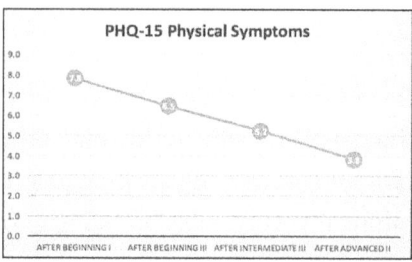

Decreased Physical Symptoms

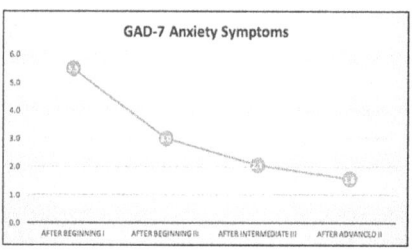

Decreased Anxiety Symptoms

A study by Bessel Van der Kolk et al. (2007), author of "The Body Keeps the Score," used fMRI to assess changes in brain activation in individuals with PTSD before and after a trauma-focused therapy, which included somatic elements. The results showed decreased activity in the amygdala and increased activation in the prefrontal cortex, indicating improved emotional regulation and reduced fear response (Van der Kolk et al., 2007). He states in his bestseller, "For many people, the only way out of their trauma is through their body." In more research conducted by Dr. David Creswell indicated somatic therapy led to increased gray matter density in regions associated with emotional regulation (Creswell et al., 2016). This study high-lighted how body-based practices promote neuroplasticity and enhance emotional resilience. In addition to this research, there have also been various case studies that offer real-life examples of the effi-cacy of somatic therapy. In this section, we'll examine three compelling case studies that highlight the transformative results of somatic therapy on individuals grappling with different types of trauma, such as childhood trauma, PTSD, and relationship trauma. Each story illustrates how these body-centered approaches can address deep-seated issues and facilitate healing in different ways.

Consider Lisa, a graphic designer in her late 30's who endured severe childhood trauma. Having grown up in a household fraught with emotional and physical abuse, she struggled with anxiety and self-destructive behaviors well into adulthood. Traditional therapies provided some relief, but nothing seemed to reach the root of her pain. Then, she discovered somatic therapy. She began to understand the origin of her pain. She used visualization and gentle self-touch to soothe her and reconnect with their body to process her trauma. Over time, these practices helped her release the deep-seated tension and fear that had plagued her for years. Lisa's story exemplifies how somatic therapy can address trauma at its root, offering hope for others with similar experiences.

Then there's Michael, a war veteran who, in his early 40s, transitioned into a role as a construction manager after serving multiple tours overseas and struggled with PTSD for years. Night-mares, flashbacks, and panic attacks were constantly plaguing him. He felt like he was living in a perpetual state of high alert, unable to relax or enjoy life. Traditional talk therapy helped him articulate his experiences, but it didn't alleviate his physical symptoms. Michael turned to somatic therapy, starting with breathwork and grounding exercises. These practices helped him regulate his nervous system, reducing the intensity of his panic attacks. By focusing on his breath and connecting with his body, Michael found a sense of calm he hadn't felt in years. His experience illustrates that even the most intense trauma can be effectively managed with the right therapeutic tools.

Emily's story is another testament to the power of somatic therapy. Emily, a social worker in her mid-30s, had endured one unhealthy relationship after another, each one eroding her trust and self-esteem. By the time she sought help, Emily felt completely disconnected from her body and emotions. She couldn't trust her own instincts, let alone another person. Somatic therapy introduced her to the concept of safe touch practices. Through guided exercises, Emily learned to experience touch in a non-threatening, nurturing way. This helped her rebuild trust not just in others but in herself. As she became more comfortable with safe touch, Emily noticed a remarkable improvement in her relationships. She felt more grounded, confident, and connected to her needs and boundaries. Emily's story serves as a testament to the personal transformation that lies within this body-centered approach.

As you read these stories, I hope you find inspiration and motivation for your own healing process, but also remember that your path to healing is unique. There is no one-size-fits-all approach, and what works for someone else might not work for you. That's all right. Trust in the process and be patient with yourself as you explore different somatic therapy techniques. Healing is not a one-time event; it's a process that requires ongoing effort.

. . .

Your story is still being written, and you have the power to shape its narrative. Whether you're dealing with childhood trauma, PTSD, relationship issues, or any other form of trauma, know that healing is possible. By engaging with somatic therapy, you're taking a proactive step towards reclaiming your well-being. You're not just a passive participant in your own life. You're actively creating a more vibrant and fulfilling life where you are capable of transforming your pain.

CORE SOMATIC TECHNIQUES FOR SELF-HEALING

"And the day came when the risk to remain tight in a bud was more painful than the risk it took to blossom."

-ANAIS NIN

In this chapter, we'll dive into the core somatic techniques designed to empower your self-healing, embodying the widely recognized idea that feeling your feelings is necessary for healing. From grounding techniques and somatic resourcing to mindful touch and gentle movement—tools that can transform your everyday experience and how you perceive and show up in this world. They're simple and accessible and you might already be familiar with some of them, especially if you already have a mindfulness or meditation practice. At first glance, they might seem too simple to actually work. Yet, they supply a double whammy of goodness. First off, when you start feeling like things are spinning out of control, these little exercise gives you back a sense of power. How? It's like turning on a light in a dark room - suddenly, you can see that you've got options and tools at your disposal. Just realizing that can be a huge relief. Plus, when you actually do the exercise, it's like hitting the reset button on your nerves. It helps you calm down and think straight. And when you're thinking clearly, you make better decisions that actually serve you well. The real kicker is that they help you avoid those facepalm moments. You know, when you say or do something in the heat of the moment and then spend the next week kicking yourself about it? Yeah, those. Making them especially handy when it comes to the people closest to you. The prominent component, however, lies in understanding when and why to use them and then incorporating them into your daily life. Think of these techniques as a set of keys. Knowing they exist is one thing, but actually using them to unlock new doors in your life is where the real transformation happens.

GROUNDING TECHNIQUES FOR STABILITY AND IMMEDIATE RELIEF

Grounding is a foundational tool in trauma recovery. It is your emotional anchor, keeping you steady when the waves of anxiety and panic threaten to capsize your boat. Grounding techniques help stabilize and calm your nervous system, bringing you back to the present moment. When you're grounded, you're less likely to be swept away by flashbacks or dissociation. Instead, you feel more connected to the here and now.

One of the easiest grounding exercises is to feel the weight of your body or your feet on the ground. (*For guided audio of these grounding exercises, please refer to the Somatic Therapy Resources at the back of this book.*)

Basic Grounding

- Stand or sit comfortably.
- Bring your attention to the sensations in your feet.
- Notice the texture of the floor beneath you.
- Feel the pressure on your soles.
- Observe how your weight shifts with each breath.

This basic act of focusing on your feet can help anchor you in the present moment, reducing anxiety and preventing dissociation.

Another instrumental technique is the "5-4-3-2-1" sensory exercise.

"5-4-3-2-1" Sensory Exercise

- Look around and name five things you can see.
- Identify four things you can touch.
- Listen for three sounds in your environment.
- Notice two smells around you.
- Focus on one thing you can taste.

5-4-3-2-1 Sensory Exercise

This exercise engages all your senses, pulling you away from distressing thoughts and grounding you in your physical surroundings. It's like hitting the refresh button on your brain, allowing you to regain control over your emotions.

If you prefer to focus on one sense at a time, try sensory exploration. For example, you might close your eyes and listen intently to the sounds around you—the hum of the refrigerator, the chirping of birds, or the distant rumble of traffic. Alternatively, you could focus on touch, feeling the texture of a smooth stone, a piece of fabric like your favorite cozy blanket, or even your own skin. Engaging in sensory exploration can provide a sense of safety and stability, helping you feel more connected and in control. You can even try placing your face in cold water or holding a piece of ice. The intense sensation can snap you out of a hyper or dissociative state and bring you back to the present moment. These strategies are also great for when you are overthinking and under-feeling, as they reduce the power of anxious or intrusive thoughts.

Scent and taste can also be used for grounding. Try smelling essential oils, like lavender or peppermint, which can have soothing or energizing properties. Or, taste something strong, like a slice of lemon or a piece of mint gum. These intense flavors and aromas can help anchor you in the present moment, also reducing anxiety and preventing dissociation.

Nature walks are another fantastic way to practice grounding. Find a quiet path and take a slow, be mindful. Pay attention to the sights, sounds, and smells around you. Feel the ground beneath your feet, the breeze on your skin, and the warmth of the sun. Strolling in nature can be incredibly soothing, helping you feel more connected to the world around you. Plus, it's a great way to get some fresh air and exercise, both of which can boost your mood.

The positive results of grounding are both emotional and physiological. Incorporating grounding techniques into your daily life can be surprisingly easy. Try grounding during work breaks, before bed, or while brushing your teeth. You can also practice grounding in social settings when going for a walk, eating, doing the dishes, or even showering. Try to make grounding a regular part of your routine so it becomes a natural way to reduce stress and anxiety.

Let's consider some real-life applications. Imagine you're about to walk into a social event that makes you anxious. Take a moment to ground yourself by feeling the weight of your feet on the ground and focusing on your breath. After experiencing a trauma trigger or flashback, use the "5-4-3-2-1" sensory exercise to reconnect with your body and the present moment. During a stressful work meeting, discreetly hold a textured object in your pocket to help you stay present and focused.

Grounding techniques are versatile, practical, and incredibly functional. The advantage of grounding is that it is available to you anywhere and at any time. These techniques provide a lifeline in moments of distress, helping you stay connected to the present moment and your body. By embedding these techniques into your daily life, you can reduce anxiety, prevent dissociation, and build emotional resilience. So, the next time you feel overwhelmed, remember you have the power to ground yourself and regain your sense of stability. You've got this.

SOMATIC RESOURCING AND VISUALIZATION: FOR EMOTIONAL RESILIENCE

Have you ever found yourself lost in a daydream, imagining a place where you feel completely safe and at peace? That's a glimpse into the power of somatic visualization. Guided imagery is a technique that uses your mind's eye to create vivid mental images, engaging all five senses to support emotional healing. Picture yourself on a serene beach: feel the warmth of the sun on your skin, hear the gentle lapping of waves, smell the salty sea air, taste the freshness in the breeze, and see the endless horizon. This immersive experience connects your mind and body, creating a sense of stability and emotional security.

Similar to visualization is resourcing. It is slightly different in that it involves tapping into your internal strengths and support systems. It's like having an emotional toolkit filled with memories, skills, and positive experiences that you can draw upon when needed. Both somatic visualization and resourcing focus on accessing internal resources, whether through direct engagement with personal strengths or by using mental imagery of reassuring and empowering scenarios. They are two sides of the same coin, aiming to build emotional resilience and provide comfort during challenging times.

Creating a safe space visualization is a combination of visualization and resourcing. (For *guided audio of these visualizations, please refer to the Somatic Therapy Resources at the back of this book.*)

Safe Space Visualization

- Find a quiet place to sit or lie down.
- Close your eyes and take a few deep breaths.
- Imagine a place where you feel completely safe and at ease (this can be real or imaginary). This could be a cozy cabin in the woods, a tranquil beach, or your childhood bedroom.
- Incorporate as many sensory details as possible:
  - **What do you see?** The soft glow of sunlight filtering through trees?
  - **What do you hear?** The gentle rustle of leaves or the distant call of birds?
  - **What do you feel?** The cool grass under your feet or the warmth of a blanket wrapped around you?
  - **What do you smell?** Fresh pine needles or blooming flowers?
  - **What do you taste?** Perhaps the sweetness of fresh fruit or the crispness of the air.

This differs from grounding because you are not taking in your current moment with all your senses but imagining a place (real or imaginary) where you feel secure, relaxed, and protected. The focus here is on creating a mental image that evokes feelings of safety and comfort, allowing you to escape stress or anxiety momentarily. By engaging all your senses, you create a vivid, immersive experience that helps your body feel safe and secure, bringing yourself back to a state of equilibrium.

Somatic visualization techniques can take various forms. An additional option is to visualize an inner resource, a symbol of strength and resilience.

. . .

Inner Resource Visualization

- Close your eyes and imagine a glowing orb of light within your chest, representing your inner strength and resilience.
- With each breath, visualize the light growing brighter and more radiant, filling your body with warmth and confidence.
- Alternatively, practice the healing light visualization:
  - Picture a warm, golden light surrounding your body.
  - Imagine this light gently soothing and healing any areas of tension or pain.
  - Visualize the light penetrating deep into your muscles, releasing any stored trauma and leaving you feeling relaxed and at peace.

Resourcing techniques are equally valuable. One option to experiment with is rooting, which involves imagining yourself as a tree to quite literally feel grounded.

Rooting Visualization

- Imagine yourself at a sturdy tree.
- See your deep, strong roots growing into the ground.
- Feel the stability and strength of these roots.
- Feel them anchoring you firmly to the earth and providing a sense of security and support.

Healing imagery exercises can further enhance emotional resilience. Visualize the release of trauma by imagining a heavy weight being lifted from your shoulders or dark clouds dispersing to reveal a clear, blue sky. You can also imagine positive outcomes, such as successfully working through a challenging situation or achieving a personal goal. These visualizations help shift your focus from fear and anxiety to hope and empowerment. It's a healthy "what if" visualization. Instead of giving into the negativity bias of worrying about all the negative "what if it doesn't," you flip the script to "what if it does work out." What if you are more successful than ever? Doesn't that feel so much better and fun to imagine? You get to choose to focus on the positive potential and imagine a wildly successful outcome.

Resourcing and visualization can reduce stress and anxiety, providing a sense of balance and control. By enhancing emotional resilience, these techniques help you manage difficult situations with greater ease. Weaving resourcing and visualization into your daily life is relatively easy. Use these techniques in high-tension situations, such as before giving a presentation or during a difficult conversation. They can also help release emotional blockages, enhance physical recovery, or assist in winding down at the end of the day.

PROGRESSIVE MUSCLE RELAXATION FOR TENSION RELEASE

After sitting at your computer all day, you may find yourself hunched over with tense shoulders and an aching back as you race to get everything done. By the time you log off, don't you feel like every part of you is drained and in desperate need of relief? Trauma can often feel that- but the tension never lets up. Progressive Muscle Relaxation (PMR) is like finally being able to step away from those endless demands and giving your muscles the break they so desperately need. PMR is a systematic technique that involves intentionally tensing and then relaxing different muscle groups in your body. This method helps release the tension stored in your muscles, offering both immediate relief and long-term benefits.

. . .

To perform PMR, find a quiet, comfortable place where you won't be disturbed. (*For guided audio of this PMR exercise, please refer to the Somatic Therapy Resources at the back of this book.*)

Progressive Muscle Relaxation (PMR)

- Start by taking a few deep breaths to center yourself.
- Begin with your feet:
  - Tense the muscles in your toes and hold for about 5 seconds, then slowly release.
  - Notice the difference between the tension and relaxation.
- Move up to your calves:
  - Tense and release.
- Proceed to your thighs:
  - Tense and release.
- Continue this process, working your way up through your body:
  - Your abdomen, then your chest.
  - Move to your arms and finally your face.

PMR isn't a one-size-fits-all practice. You can modify it to suit your needs. If you're short on time, try a quick mini PMR session focusing on just a few muscle groups, like your shoulders, neck, and jaw—areas where tension often accumulates. For a more profound, more comprehensive session, dedicate 10-30 minutes to go through all the muscle groups from head to toe. Some people find it helpful to use guided PMR recordings, which can provide structure and help you stay focused. YouTube is an excellent resource if you would prefer a more detailed guided PMR.

· · ·

The benefits of PMR are both physical and psychological as well. Regular practice can significantly reduce muscle tension, helping you feel more relaxed and at ease. As you become more aware of when tension begins to build, you can interrupt this pattern using Progressive Muscle Relaxation (PMR). It can also improve your sleep quality by helping you unwind before bed, reducing the tossing and turning that often accompany anxiety and stress. By releasing physical tension, PMR helps alleviate emotional stress, yet again creating a sense of restoration and well-being.

To get the most out of PMR, create a conducive environment. Find a quiet space where you can relax without interruptions. Dim the lights, play some soft music if you would like, or use a white noise machine if it helps you focus. Consistency matters, so try to practice PMR at the same time each day. It may be conducive to integrating PMR into your bedtime routine, making it easier to drift off to sleep.

In real-life applications, PMR can be an excellent remedy. Before tackling a busy day of managing family schedules and work demands, take a few minutes to tense and relax your muscles, mellowing your nerves and improving your focus. After a stressful day, use PMR to unwind and release the tension that has built up in your body. It's like hitting the reset button, allowing you to start fresh with a clear mind and relaxed body.

Remember, the goal of PMR is to cultivate awareness and support a relaxed state. It's okay if your mind wanders or you don't feel completely relaxed after every session. The rewards of PMR build over time, so be patient with yourself and stay committed to the practice. Your body will thank you for it.

GENTLE MOVEMENT AND DANCE THERAPY PRACTICES FOR EMOTIONAL EXPRESSION AND PROCESSING

Do you know how when you are driving, and your favorite song comes on and you can't help but start dancing and singing along? You're not worried about how you look; you're in the moment and feeling that song, maybe even belting it out at the top of your lungs. That's the beauty of somatic movement. It's all about the internal experience, not the external performance. Somatic movement focuses on the sensations within your body, helping you flush out stress chemicals like cortisol and trigger endorphins—those feel-good hormones we covered that act as natural painkillers. It's a practice that encourages you to move in ways that feel good to your body, respecting any physical limitations and discomfort. The goal is to enhance your body awareness and regulate your nervous system, not to achieve perfect form or impress anyone.

By paying attention to how your body feels as you move, you become more attuned to your physical and emotional states. This heightened awareness can help you identify and release stored tension and emotions, often ones you didn't even realize were there. When you move mindfully, you activate the parasympathetic nervous system, which induces relaxation and reduces stress. It's an innate way to reinvigorate your body and mind, making it easier to deal with the complexities of trauma.

There are various movement-based techniques to explore. Cathartic movement, for example, can involve shaking out your body to release pent-up energy or using the "throw it out" method, where you visualize emotions as physical objects, and throw them away while exhaling, combining physical action with emotional release.

. . .

Shake It Out

- Stand up and plant your feet firmly on the ground.
- Start shaking your hands, then your arms, and finally your whole body.
- Let go of any tension and feel the energy flow.
- Try bouncing on the balls of your feet or partially shifting your weight from one foot to the other if that feels right.
- Continue until you feel it's time to stop.

Shake It Out

Throw It Out

- Raise your arms up and out in front of you as if you are holding an oversized beach ball.
- Slightly bend your knees.
- Pretend to throw it down to the ground and complete the motion by allowing your arms to swing back behind you.
- This can be done gently and rhythmically or more intensely to release feelings of anger or frustration. You can imagine you are throwing away whatever is bothering you.
- Repeat until you feel it's time to stop.

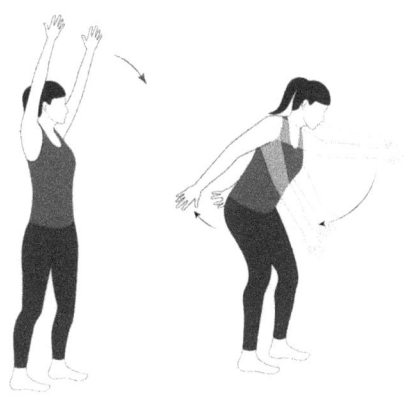

Throw It Out

Another option is to engage in dance and free movement to express your emotions through spontaneous, uninhibited movement. Gently sway back and forth, beautifully flail about. Put on your favorite music and let your body move however it wants to move. Let it be goofy; let it be sultry. Rock out if you want to. Do what your body needs to do. Don't think about what it looks like. Don't think about it at all. Close your eyes and let your body move itself to the music.

Think more interpretive dance than choreography. Don't worry about looking graceful; focus on feeling free. This may feel really awkward at first, and it is best to do it in a place where you can be alone and uninterrupted so you can give yourself time and really let loose if your body will allow.

Yoga poses are another excellent option for gentle movement. Poses like child's pose, cat-cow, downward dog, and warrior II are specifically great for connecting with your body and releasing tension, whether you are a beginner or a yogi. Tai Chi, with its slow, flowing movements, also offers a meditative way to engage in gentle movement. These movements invite you to move mindfully, directing your attention to the internal experience rather than the external appearance.

Yoga Poses

More sequenced practices can provide structure and support as you engage in gentle movement. For example, you can start with a basic warm-up.

Gentle Movement Sequence

- Stand with your feet hip-width apart, and take a few deep breaths.
- Begin to sway gently from side to side, letting your arms hang loose.
- Gradually increase the intensity, and add in more exaggerated movements like arm circles or gentle twists.
- Feel free to turn on some music if that helps. Then, transition into a free dance, allowing your body to move intuitively to the music if that invitation feels good.
- Finish with a cool-down, returning to gentle swaying and deep breathing. This sequence helps you connect with your body, release tension, and feel more grounded.

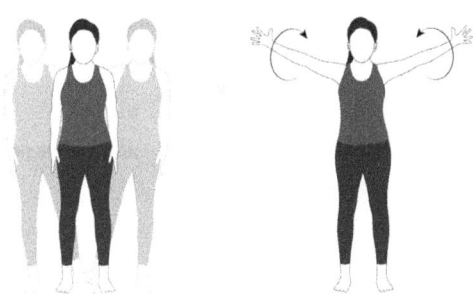

Gentle Movement

There are countless real-life applications for movement and dance therapy. Use these practices when you're feeling overwhelmed or stuck as a way to process emotions and regain your sense of stability. For example, if you're dealing with a stressful family situation, take a few minutes to step away and move your body. Shake out the tension, do a few yoga poses, or take a walk. These little actions can feel like an emotional cleansing; if you're struggling with intense emotions like anger or feeling moody, put on some music and dance it out. Letting your body express your feelings aids in the release of suppressed emotions. These practices offer an approachable way to reconnect with yourself, shake loose pent-up emotions, and handle the ups and downs of life.

THE BODY SCAN: MINDFUL OBSERVATION AND SELF-AWARENESS

Imagine lying down after a long, stressful day. Your mind is racing, and you can't seem to relax. This is where body scanning can be convenient. Body scanning is a technique used in somatic therapy to increase bodily awareness and identify areas of tension similar to PMR. It's like a mental X-ray, helping you tune into the subtleties of your body. By doing a body scan, you can pinpoint where you hold stress and begin to release it. It's an exercise in mindful observation, allowing you to notice sensations without judgment.

Start by finding a comfortable position, either lying down or sitting. (*For guided audio of this body scan, please refer to the Somatic Therapy Resources at the back of this book.*)

Body Scan

- Close your eyes and take a few deep breaths.
- Begin at your toes, bringing your attention to any sensations you feel.

- o Are they warm or cool?
- o Relaxed or tense?
- Slowly move up to your ankles and calves, observing any tension or pain.
- Continue this process, moving through your knees, thighs, hips, and so on.
- When you reach your head, take a moment to observe your entire body.
- Notice any areas that stand out.
  - o Are there emotional connections to these sensations?
  - o Reflect on this without judgment.
- Finally, end your body scan with a grounding exercise to bring yourself back to the present moment.

Body scanning is versatile. If you're short on time, try a mini-scan like with PMR, focusing on specific body parts like your shoulders, neck, and jaw—the areas infamously known to accumulate tension. A quick 5-minute body scan can be done almost anytime, anywhere. The goal is to make it a habitual practice.

Routine practice can amplify restfulness, making it easier to unwind and let go of stress, which is ideal in many situations. It also improves self-awareness, helping you become more attuned to your body and its needs. This heightened awareness can lead to better health as you learn to address issues before they become chronic problems.

Implementing body scanning into your daily life is easy. Make it part of your morning routine to start the day with a sense of calm and focus. Use it during breaks at work to relieve stress and refocus. A pre-sleep body scan can help you relax and improve sleep quality. Consider waking up and spending a few minutes scanning your body before getting out of bed. Notice how you feel, and address any areas of tension with gentle stretches or mindful breathing. Do this day or night to release physical and emotional stress. These small, consistent practices will make a major difference in how you feel.

MINDFUL TOUCH AND SELF-MASSAGE TECHNIQUES TO SELF SOOTHE

Self-massage is a form of mindful touch that can provide immense comfort and relief, especially for those who've experienced trauma. It's about safe, intentional touch that soothes and comforts, helping to alleviate chronic pain and emotional stress. This may sound overly basic because you may commonly give your shoulder a few squeezes as a reaction to tight muscles to seek relief on occasion. However, self-massage in this context refers to the practice of self-massage and touch done in a more mindful and intentional way. This is more of a self-care practice that allows you to connect with your body in a healthy way. Let's start with some basic self-massage techniques.

Basic Self Massage

- Sit comfortably. For your scalp and neck, use your fingertips to make small, circular motions across your scalp and the back of your neck. For your neck and shoulders, place your right hand on your left shoulder.
- Gently squeeze and release the muscles, working your way from your shoulder to the base of your neck.
- Switch sides and repeat.
- For your hands and forearms, use your thumb to apply gentle pressure in circular motions, starting from your wrist and moving toward your fingers.
- Finally, For your feet, sit comfortably and use both hands to knead the arch of each foot, applying gentle pressure with your thumbs.

. . .

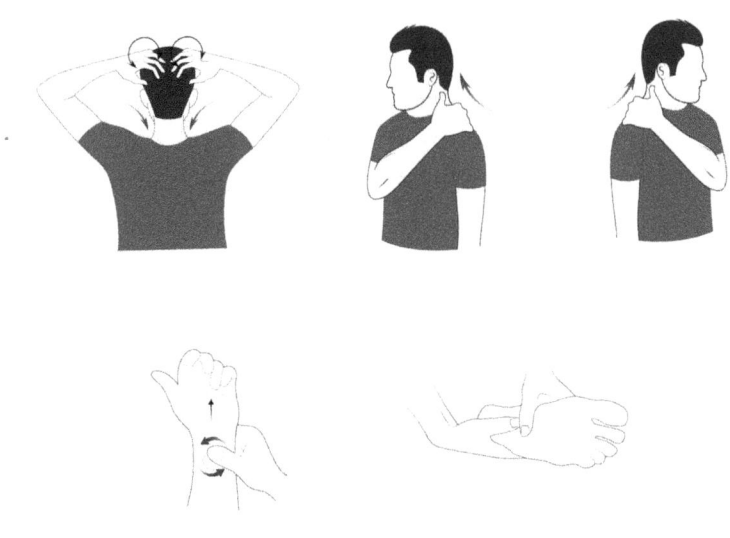

Self Massage

These basic techniques can provide immediate relief and help you feel more connected to yourself.

Therapeutic tools like foam rollers and massage balls can enhance your self-massage practice and are excellent for targeting specific areas of tension. For example, to use a foam roller for back pain, lie on your back with the foam roller positioned under your upper back. Slowly roll up and down, allowing the roller to massage your muscles. Massage balls can be used similarly for more precise pressure. Place the ball between your back and a wall, and gently roll to find and release tight spots. These tools can intensify the massage experience, providing greater relief and soothing effects.

. . .

Mindful touch and self-massage extend beyond physical relief to help reduce stress and make you feel more mellow by activating the body's relaxation response. When you do so, you're sending a signal to your body that it's safe to unwind. This can help regulate your emotions, providing a nurturing experience that allows you to process and release stored emotions. It's like giving yourself a gentle hug, reminding your body and mind that they are cared for and valued, which is also something you can do, literally.

Creating a self-massage routine can be a rewarding addition to your self-care practices. Start by setting aside a few minutes each day for self-massage. You might combine it with other somatic practices, like deep breathing or grounding exercises, to create a comprehensive routine. To stay consistent, make it a habit, whether it's part of your morning routine to start the day relaxed or a bedtime ritual to unwind. Over time, you'll find that consistent self-massage helps you feel more connected to your body and better able to cope with stress.

Incorporating self-massage into your everyday life is straightforward. You don't need any special equipment or extensive training—just your hands and a few minutes of your time. Whether you're sitting at your desk feeling overwhelmed or lying in bed at night, these techniques are accessible and effective. They provide a moment of respite, a chance to reconnect with your body and offer it the care and attention it deserves.

BREATHING TECHNIQUES FOR NERVOUS SYSTEM REGULATION

Imagine you're sitting in traffic. The car ahead hasn't moved in ages, and you can feel your stress levels rising. This is a great opportunity to engage in some breathwork, a straightforward yet powerful tool. Breathwork, or controlled breathing, contributes to trauma recovery by engaging your diaphragm and activating the parasympathetic nervous system—the part that signals, "Hey, it's okay to relax now." When you breathe deeply, you stimulate the vagus nerve, which helps even out your body's stress responses. Shallow breathing, often a default under stress, keeps you in a fight-or-flight mode. Deep breathing, however, signals your body to reset and go into digest mode.

Diaphragmatic breathing, also known as deep breathing, is an easy way to reboot your system. (*For guided audio of these breathing exercises, please refer to the Somatic Therapy Resources at the back of this book.*)

Diaphragmatic (Deep) Breathing

- Start by sitting comfortably, placing one hand on your chest and the other on your abdomen.
- Inhale deeply through your nose, allowing your abdomen to rise while keeping your chest still.
- Exhale slowly through your mouth, feeling your abdomen fall.
- Repeat this for a few minutes or as many times as you need.

Diaphragmatic breathing not only lowers stress but also improves oxygen flow, helping you feel more energized and focused.

. . .

Paced breathing techniques offer structured ways to manage stress—particularly the 4-7-8 breathing and box breathing techniques, which are excellent for immediate calming.

4-7-8 Breathing

- Inhale through your nose for a count of four.
- Hold your breath for a count of seven.
- Exhale through your mouth for a count of eight.
- This method is especially useful before bed to help transition into sleep or during moments of acute stress.

Box Breathing

- Inhale for four seconds.
- Hold for four seconds.
- Exhale for four seconds.
- Hold again for four seconds.

This technique is useful for relaxation and focus, making it perfect for high-pressure situations like a medical emergency or before a job interview or financial negotiation. For a more versatile approach, try alternate nostril breathing.

Alternate Nostril Breathing

- Sit comfortably and use your right thumb to close your right nostril.
- Inhale deeply through your left nostril.
- Close your left nostril with your right ring finger and release your thumb to open your right nostril.
- Exhale through your right nostril.

- Inhale through your right nostril, then close it.
- Open left nostril and exhale through your left nostril.
- Repeat this cycle for a 1-3 minutes.

Alternate Nostril Breathing

Alternate nostril breathing centers the nervous system, making it ideal for reducing anxiety and enhancing focus.

Breath of Fire, a more invigorating technique, involves rapid, rhythmic breathing.

Breath of Fire

- Start by sitting comfortably.
- Quickly inhale and exhale through your nose, keeping your breaths short and equal. (about 1 second per breath)
- Make sure your abdomen pumps with each breath.
- Continue this pattern for 30 seconds to a minute.

This technique can increase energy and improve mental clarity, making it great for a mid-afternoon slump or before a workout.

· · ·

Mindful breathwork reduces stress and brings about a sense of ease by activating the parasympathetic nervous system, lowering heart rate and blood pressure. Breathwork also helps regulate the autonomic nervous system, shifting you from a stress-inducing sympathetic response to a restorative parasympathetic state. It can be a lifeline during stressful or overwhelming situations. Use it whenever you need to chill out, whether at a red light, before bed, or as part of your daily self-care practice. When you have a very busy week and feel the tension rise, remember to "take a breather." A few rounds of 4-7-8 breathing can help you regain focus and composure. Or, before drifting off to sleep, a diaphragmatic breathing session can ease you into a restful slumber.

TITRATION AND PENDULATION TO PROCESS STORED TRAUMA

Imagine the body as a container, holding all the stress, emotions, and traumas you've ever experienced. Over time, this container can start to overflow, leading to physical and emotional distress. Somatic Experiencing® (SE™), developed by Peter Levine, offers a way to release this stored trauma, allowing you to find security and peace. Levine's approach focuses on the body, recognizing that trauma isn't just an event that happens in the mind but an experience that lives in your tissues and nervous system.

While these techniques are a slightly more more advanced than the earlier methods, they are still fitting for a solo practice. The first technique in this approach is pendulation, which involves shifting between states of tension and relaxation. Think of it as dipping your toe in and out of a hot tub, gradually acclimating to the temperature. This method helps you build resilience by experiencing small doses of distress followed by periods of comfort. It teaches your nervous system to move through these intense emotions without getting stuck.

(For guided audio of these exercises, please refer to the Somatic Therapy Resources at the back of this book.)

Pendulation

- Find a comfortable position and sit or lie down in a quiet space where you feel safe and undisturbed.
- Take a few deep breaths, inhaling deeply through your nose and allowing your belly to expand. Exhale slowly through your mouth. Repeat a few times to settle into the moment.
- Tune into your body by closing your eyes if you're comfortable and bring your awareness to your body. Notice how you feel physically and emotionally.
- Identify a comfortable sensation and focus on a part of your body where you feel comfortable or relaxed. This could be your feet, hands, or a specific area that feels good. Notice the sensations there.
- Allow yourself to feel this sensation and stay with this comfortable sensation for a few moments.
  - Really immerse yourself in it—what does it feel like?
  - Is there warmth, heaviness, or a sense of ease?
- Shift to a less comfortable sensation. Now, gently bring your awareness to an area that feels tense or uncomfortable. It could be tight shoulders, a heavy stomach, or any place of discomfort. Don't force it; just notice it.
- Alternate between sensations by moving back and forth between the comfortable sensation and the uncomfortable one. Spend a few moments with each, allowing your body to experience both without judgment.
- End with a grounding exercise or some deep breathing.

Another key technique is titration, which breaks down traumatic memories into manageable pieces. Instead of diving headfirst into a sea of painful memories, you take it one drop at a time, making the process less overwhelming. When first trying this technique, start with a memory that feels slightly moderate and not too intense so you can slowly and gently engage with your emotions without getting too consumed.

Titration

- Start by getting comfortable, sitting or lying down in a quiet place where you feel safe.
- Take deep breaths, inhaling through your nose and exhaling slowly through your mouth a few times to center yourself.
- Close your eyes if you're comfortable, and notice how your body feels physically and emotionally.
- Focus on a mild discomfort in your body, like tension in your neck or tightness in your stomach, and acknowledge it.
- Spend a moment observing this discomfort—how it feels and where it is.
- Recall a brief memory related to this discomfort that feels safe to think about.
- Shift your attention back to your breath and take a few deep breaths to relax.
- Focus on a positive sensation in your body, like your feet on the floor or relaxation in your hands. Notice this for a moment.
- Alternate between the memory and the positive sensation, spending a few moments on each.
- Pay attention to any changes in your body or emotions as you do this.
- Ground yourself by feeling your feet on the floor and your body supported.
- End the exercise with a few deep breaths, bringing your

awareness back to the room. Open your eyes when you're ready.
- Take a moment to reflect on how you feel, and if you would like, jot down any insights or sensations you noticed

These experiencing exercises allow you to process specific sensations and memories in a manageable way while keeping your emotional state regulated.

These exercises are beneficial because they help process emotions through incremental exposure; you can gradually reduce the intensity of traumatic memories. This approach helps regulate emotional states, allowing you to tolerate fluctuations in your feelings and physiological responses. Over time, you build a higher capacity for resilience, making it easier to handle stress and anxiety.

In everyday scenarios, titration and pendulation can be incredibly useful. Imagine you're at a social event, feeling overwhelmed by the crowd. Instead of withdrawing, use pendulation to shift your focus between the tension in your body and a stabilizing breath. This helps you stay present without becoming overwhelmed. During moments of stress or anxiety, practice tracking internal sensations. Focus on a neutral or pleasant area of your body, such as your hands or feet, to ground yourself and reduce the intensity of your emotions. These techniques provide more practical tools for daily life, helping you feel more in control and less at the mercy of your past. As you incorporate these practices into your life, you'll find that they become second nature, providing a steady foundation for healing that honors the wisdom of your body.

Unlock the Power of Healing Through Sharing

"Your words have the power to change lives—yours and others."

- Unknown

Sharing our experiences creates a ripple effect of positivity. Let's make a difference together!

Would you help someone curious about Somatic Therapy but unsure where to start? Your input could have a meaningful impact on reaching more people.

Most readers choose books based on reviews. By leaving a review, you can help someone searching for answers. It costs nothing and takes less than a minute. Your review could help:

...one more person feel at home in their body.

...one more person find relief from their past.

...one more reader navigate their emotions.

...one more soul connect with their inner strength.

To make a difference, simply scan the QR code below and leave a review:

Scan to Review

Thank you from the bottom of my heart! 🩶

TAILORING SOMATIC THERAPY TO SPECIFIC TYPES OF TRAUMA

"Never be ashamed of a scar; it means you were stronger than whatever tried to hurt you."

-UNKNOWN

Trauma can take many forms, and in this chapter, we will delve into various types of trauma, including childhood, PTSD, complex trauma, physical trauma, sexual trauma, and relationship trauma. We will focus on these five specific types because they're prevalent and encompass a wide range of trauma experiences that many people face, making it easier to develop a targeted approach. As you read through each description, keep in mind that you might relate to one type or find echoes of multiple experiences within your story. Each section will cover the unique characteristics, trauma responses, and common struggles, then highlight techniques best suited for each. That said, please do not feel limited to the suggested techniques; they are just guidelines and are provided to give you a place to start when creating your personal practice. Allow your body and intuition to guide you toward what feels best for you and lead you to greater clarity and confidence.

CHILDHOOD TRAUMA

Imagine you're sitting in a crowded restaurant, enjoying dinner with friends, when a plate crashes to the floor, shattering loudly. In an instant, your body tenses, your heart races, and your breath becomes shallow. The lively chatter fades into a distant buzz as you're transported back to childhood moments when sudden noises meant danger. Your friends continue talking, oblivious to your distress, but you struggle to focus. Your hands shake as you grip the table, fighting the urge to flee to a safe place. You know, logically, that you're safe now, but your body reacts as if you're in real danger. This is the reality of living with childhood trauma; even in ordinary situations, the past can intrude, reminding you that healing is an ongoing journey. This is how childhood trauma can make you feel—like the familiar has become a minefield. If you've ever felt like this, you're not alone.

Childhood trauma is a beast of its own. It sneaks into the formative years when your brain is still developing, making its impression both deep and wide. Unlike trauma experienced in adulthood, childhood trauma can shape the very foundation of your emotional world. It's like building a house on shaky ground; every structure you erect afterward is affected. The repercussions can be devastating, affecting everything from self-esteem to physical health.

Emotionally, childhood trauma often manifests as anxiety and depression. You might feel a constant undercurrent of worry, a sense that something bad is always about to happen. Depression can follow you like a shadow, casting a pall over your daily life. Low self-esteem is another common outcome. When the people who were supposed to protect and nurture you fail to do so, it sends a message that you're not worth protecting. This can lead to attachment issues, making it hard to form meaningful relationships and trust others. You might find yourself keeping people at arm's length, afraid to let anyone get too close.

Physically, the toll of childhood trauma can be equally substantial. Chronic pain, headaches, and digestive problems are common complaints. It's as if your body is carrying the weight of your past, manifesting emotional pain as physical symptoms. Fatigue is another frequent companion. When your nervous system is constantly in overdrive, it's no wonder you feel exhausted all the time. Your body is expending a tremendous amount of energy just to keep you functioning.

Behaviorally, childhood trauma can lead to difficulties with boundaries. You might find it hard to say no, to stand up for yourself, or even to know where your boundaries lie. Compulsive behaviors can become a coping mechanism, a way to exert control in an uncontrollable world. You might also struggle with unhealthy attachment styles. Whether you cling too tightly to others or push them away, these patterns can make it challenging to form and maintain healthy relationships. Yet, people who've experienced childhood trauma often develop remarkable adaptive characteristics, including resilience and creativity. It's the silver lining of your suffering. You've learned to maneuver through a world that hasn't always been kind to you, and this has given you strengths that you might not even recognize. However, these strengths can come with struggles, particularly with self-regulation, attachment, and trust issues. The very mechanisms that helped you survive can become obstacles to thriving.

. . .

Techniques best suited for addressing childhood trauma often start with body awareness and mindfulness. Introducing breathing exercises can deepen this awareness, helping you center yourself, while safe space imagery allows you to visualize a nurturing environment that fosters comfort and resilience. These practices help you reconnect with bodily sensations and develop a sense of safety and grounding, guiding you back to yourself. Mindfulness teaches you to observe your thoughts and feelings without judgment, creating a space where healing can occur. Movement and dance are also great resources as they inspire self-expression and help release suppressed emotions. Imagine dancing away your pain, each movement a step toward liberation.

Mindful touch and self-massage are particularly nourishing for those healing from neglect or abuse. These practices cultivate relaxation and body awareness, helping you reclaim a sense of ownership over your physical self. It's as if you're telling your body, "I'm here. I see you. We're safe now." The act of gently massaging your own shoulders or feet can be profoundly soothing, a way to nurture yourself in a world that may have been harsh and unkind.

The desired outcomes of these techniques are manifold. Improved self-regulation means you're better equipped to handle stress and emotional triggers. Increased self-esteem leads to a more positive relationship with yourself and those around you. Healthier relationships become possible as you learn to trust and set boundaries. Ultimately, these practices aim to create a sense of safety and stability, both within yourself and in your interactions with the world.

. . .

Childhood trauma is like a devastating storm that leaves a lasting impact, but with the right tools, you can rebuild. By engaging in somatic practices suited to your unique experiences, you're not just surviving—you're taking steps toward thriving. Each mindful breath, each gentle touch, and each joyful dance brings you closer to a life where you feel safe, valued, and whole. Despite what you have experienced in the past and what led you here, know that healing now is not just possible; it's within your reach.

PTSD (POST-TRAUMATIC STRESS DISORDER)

PTSD—Post-Traumatic Stress Disorder is triggered by an event so overwhelming that it leaves a lasting imprint on your psyche. It's more than just a set of bad memories; it's a condition that hijacks your emotional and physical well-being. PTSD can stem from various traumatic experiences, including, but not limited to, personal assaults or abuse, military combat, or natural disasters. It's characterized by severe anxiety, flashbacks, nightmares, and irritability. You might find yourself on edge, feeling emotionally numb yet overwhelmed by intense emotions.

Physically, PTSD takes a toll on your body. Chronic stress symptoms such as increased heart rate and sweating become the norm. Sleep disturbances plague your nights, and muscle tension never entirely leaves your body. It's like your body is always in fight-or-flight mode, preparing for a danger that never seems to pass. These physical symptoms make it hard to relax, contributing to a cycle of stress and anxiety that feels impossible to break.

Behaviorally, PTSD often manifests as avoidance of reminders of the traumatic event. You might go out of your way to avoid places, people, or situations that trigger painful memories. Hypervigilance, or being constantly on alert, becomes second nature. This heightened state of awareness can make it difficult to concentrate, as your mind is continually scanning for potential threats. It's as if you're living in a war zone, even when you're in the safety of your own home.

Despite these challenges, individuals with PTSD often develop impressive adaptive traits. You may have honed coping strategies that help you manage daily life, showing resilience in the face of adversity. These coping mechanisms are like battle scars, proof of your strength and ability to survive. However, these strategies can also become obstacles. Hypervigilance, while protective, can keep you in a state of constant anxiety. Avoidance behaviors, while initially comforting, can isolate you and prevent you from fully engaging with life.

A really practical technique for managing PTSD is breathwork. Breathwork helps to soothe the nervous system and reduce physical symptoms of stress. By focusing on your breath, you can activate the parasympathetic nervous system, signaling to your body that it's okay to relax. Try a quick 4-7-8 breathing exercise. Repeat this a few times, and notice how your body starts to feel more at ease.

These regulated processing methods are another option for those dealing with PTSD. This technique allows you to gradually process traumatic memories while regulating your nervous system. Unlike traditional therapies that may require you to relive the trauma, titration and pendulation focus on bodily sensations. By paying attention to how your body feels, you can release stored tension and trauma. It's like slowly deflating a balloon, letting out the pressure bit by bit until it's manageable.

. . .

Grounding techniques also play a crucial role in managing PTSD. These techniques help create a sense of stability and safety, anchoring you in the present moment. When you feel a flashback or panic attack coming on, grounding can be a lifesaver. Simple actions like placing your feet firmly on the ground, holding a textured object, or focusing on your breath can help you stay connected to the here and now. Grounding is like a mental anchor, preventing you from being swept away by the tides of trauma.

The desired outcomes of these techniques are substantial. By adding breathwork, gradual exposure techniques, and grounding into your daily routine, you can reduce symptoms of anxiety and hypervigilance. Improved emotional regulation means you're better equipped to handle stress and emotional triggers. Better management of traumatic memories allows you to reclaim your life, reducing the power these memories hold over you. Imagine waking up and feeling a sense of ease, knowing that you have the tools to face whatever the day brings. This is not just a dream; it's a possibility when you engage with somatic practices tailored to your needs.

Engaging with these techniques can help you take control of your healing process. You're not just a passive recipient of care; you're an active participant in your own recovery. Each breath, each grounding exercise, and each moment of gradual exposure brings you closer to a life where PTSD no longer dictates your every move. So take a deep breath, feel your feet on the ground, and know that healing is not just a distant hope—it's within your grasp.

COMPLEX TRAUMA

Unlike single-incident trauma, which stems from one event, complex trauma results from chronic, multiple traumas. These are often interpersonal and occur over an extended period, such as ongoing emotional abuse, neglect, or living in a war zone. Complex trauma is often linked with childhood trauma. The cumulative effect can be overwhelming, creating a tangled web of emotional, physical, and behavioral reactions.

Complex trauma can leave you feeling like your life is a perpetual storm with no safe harbor in sight. Emotionally, it can manifest as pervasive feelings of helplessness and despair. You might find it difficult to regulate your emotions, swinging between intense anger and overwhelming sadness. Relationships often become battlegrounds as trust issues and attachment problems rear their ugly heads. It's like trying to build a house on quicksand; no matter how hard you try, stability remains elusive.

Physically, the impact of complex trauma is far-reaching. Chronic pain, fatigue, and a host of other stress-related symptoms become your constant companions. Imagine waking up every day feeling like you've run a marathon, even though you barely left your bed. Your body carries the weight of your experiences, manifesting emotional pain as physical symptoms. Digestive issues, frequent headaches or migraines, and muscle tension are all part of the package, adding another layer of complexity to your already challenging life.

Behaviorally, complex trauma can lead to a range of maladaptive coping mechanisms. You might find yourself engaging in self-destructive behaviors, like substance abuse or self-harm, as a way to numb the pain. Boundaries become blurred, making it difficult to protect yourself or assert your needs. Unhealthy attachment styles often develop, leading to codependent or avoidant relationship patterns. It's like trying to find your way in a maze with no map, constantly bumping into walls and dead ends.

Despite these challenges, individuals with complex trauma often exhibit remarkable resilience and resourcefulness. You've learned to survive in an environment that was anything but safe, developing coping strategies that, while not always healthy, helped you get through the day. These adaptive traits are strengths that can be harnessed for healing. However, the same mechanisms that helped you survive can become obstacles to thriving. Struggles with self-regulation, attachment, and trust issues can make it difficult to move forward.

One advantageous technique for addressing complex trauma is body awareness paired with mindfulness. These practices help you reconnect with your body and develop a sense of safety. By tuning into your physical sensations, you can start to identify and release the tension stored in your body. Imagine lying down and performing a body scan, noticing areas of tightness and consciously relaxing them. As straightforward as this is, it can be incredible for grounding you in the present moment and providing a sense of relief.

Movement and dance can also be transformative for complex trauma because they center around expressing your feelings with your body to release suppressed emotions that are often difficult to articulate. Picture yourself in a room with music playing, moving freely, and letting your body do as it sees fit. Each movement becomes a form of release, a way to process and let go of the pain. This is not about performing a perfect dance; it's about allowing your body to communicate and heal.

Pendulation and titration are invaluable techniques for those healing from complex trauma, as they facilitate a nuanced approach to processing difficult emotions and memories. By alternating between distressing sensations and moments of safety, pendulation allows you to gradually engage with your trauma without becoming overwhelmed. This process promotes emotional regulation and builds resilience. Similarly, titration helps in breaking down traumatic experiences into smaller, manageable pieces, which can prevent the flood of overwhelming emotions that often accompany complex trauma. These methods create a sense of control and safety in the healing process, enabling you to reclaim a sense of agency by fostering a safer internal environment. This approach is great for helping to rewire the brain's response to trauma, sending a reassuring message to your nervous system: "I can explore my past while staying safe in my body."

All of these techniques improve self-regulation, enabling you to handle stress and emotional triggers more skillfully. As a result, you develop increased self-esteem and a healthier relationship with yourself. This newfound self-awareness allows you to set boundaries and build trust, developing healthier relationships with others. Ultimately, these practices aim to create a sense of safety and stability, both internally and in your interactions with the world.

Complex trauma may have shaped you, but it doesn't define you. By engaging in somatic practices aligned with your unique experiences, you're transforming your life from one of mere endurance to one of growth and flourishing. Each mindful breath, each gentle touch, and each joyful dance brings you closer to a life where you feel safe, valued, and whole.

PHYSICAL TRAUMA

When you've experienced physical trauma, the emotional fallout can be overwhelming. Fear and anxiety become constant companions, often linked directly to the abuse, injury, or the event itself. You might find yourself replaying the incident in your mind, each time feeling the same surge of panic or dread. Post-traumatic stress related to the injury or abuse can make you hyper-aware of your body, constantly on the lookout for signs of pain or re-injury. This heightened sense of vigilance can be exhausting, leaving you feeling drained and on edge.

Physically, the repercussions of trauma can be equally daunting. Pain becomes a daily reality, sometimes localized to the injury site but often spreading to other areas as your body compensates. Limited mobility can make even small tasks feel monumental, interfering with your ability to work, exercise, or enjoy hobbies. Chronic fatigue sets in as your body expends immense energy just to cope with the ongoing stress. Muscle tension becomes a permanent fixture, a constant reminder of the trauma your body endured. It's like carrying around an invisible weight that never lets up.

Behaviorally, you might find yourself avoiding physical activity altogether, fearful of triggering pain or worsening your condition. Hyper-awareness of the injury site can make you overly cautious, limiting your movements and activities. This avoidance can lead to a sedentary lifestyle, which only exacerbates the physical symptoms. It's a vicious cycle where the fear of pain leads to inactivity, which in turn leads to more pain and decreased mobility.

However, those who've faced physical trauma often develop incredible grit and ingenuity. You've learned to navigate a world that suddenly feels dangerous and unpredictable. Especially if your injury has impacted your body in some limiting way- you've likely had to discover new and creative ways to operate day to day. This perseverance is a testament to your inner strength. Yet, this resilience can come with its own set of challenges. Physical limitations can erode your self-esteem, making you feel less capable or less worthy. Fear of re-injury can become a challenging hurdle, preventing you from fully engaging in life.

Breathwork should not be underestimated for managing the pain and stress associated with physical trauma. By focusing on your breath, you can activate the parasympathetic nervous system, which is great for relaxation and pain reduction. Imagine sitting quietly, taking slow, deep breaths, and feeling the tension in your body begin to melt away. Breathwork is not just about breathing; it's about reclaiming control over your body's responses. It's a small yet productive way to manage pain and stress, helping you feel more settled and in control.

Progressive Muscle Relaxation (PMR) is another recommended technique. By systematically tensing and then relaxing different muscle groups, PMR helps release chronic muscle tension and pain. Picture yourself lying down, starting with your feet, and moving up through your body, tensing each muscle group for a few seconds before releasing. As you work your way up, you'll notice a gradual sense of relaxation spreading through your body. PMR is like giving your muscles permission to let go, to release the tension they've been holding onto.

Dance and gentle movement can also play an important role in your recovery. While it might seem counterintuitive to engage in physical activity when you're in pain, gradual re-engagement with movement can help improve mobility and reduce pain. Start with gentle, low-impact movements, such as stretching or slow walking. As your confidence and strength build, you can add more dynamic movements, like dancing. Movement and dance let you express yourself freely and help you let go of suppressed emotions, fostering a sense of freedom and joy.

Reduced pain means you can engage more fully in daily activities without the constant burden of discomfort. Improved mobility allows you to reclaim your independence, doing the things you love without fear of pain or injury. Increased comfort and confidence in physical activities open up new possibilities, whether it's taking a walk in the park, dancing at a party, or simply playing with your kids. These outcomes are not just about physical recovery; they're about reclaiming your life and your sense of self. Engaging with these somatic practices geared towards physical trauma can help you confront the challenges you face. Each breath, each moment of ease, each step of movement brings you closer to a life where pain no longer defines you.

SEXUAL TRAUMA

Sexual trauma is a specific form of physical trauma. It's not just about the moment of violation but the aftermath that lingers, permeating through every facet of your life. Sexual trauma occurs when an individual experiences non-consensual, coercive, abusive, or violent sexual acts. This can include harassment, exploitation, and manipulation, each leaving a lasting imprint on your well-being. The emotional toll of sexual trauma is immense. Shame and guilt often become unwelcome companions, whispering lies that it was somehow your fault. Depression and anxiety follow close behind, making basic daily tasks feel insurmountable. Difficulties with intimacy can arise, turning what should be moments of connection into sources of anxiety.

Physically, sexual trauma can manifest in ways that are both debilitating and confusing. Sexual dysfunction is a common issue, making physical intimacy challenging or even painful. Chronic pain, particularly in the pelvic region, can serve as a constant reminder of the trauma. Tension in this area can make you feel like your body is betraying you. It's as if your muscles have taken on the role of protector, remaining vigilant and tight long after the danger has passed. These physical symptoms can be particularly isolating, as they are often invisible to others, making it hard to explain why you're hurting.

Behaviorally, sexual trauma can lead to avoidance of sexual activity altogether. The thought of intimacy might trigger flashbacks or panic attacks, leading you to avoid not just physical closeness but emotional intimacy as well. Hypervigilance becomes a way of life as you constantly scan your environment for potential threats. Trust becomes a rare commodity, making relationships difficult to maintain. It's like living with a constant sense of dread, never fully able to relax or let your guard down.

Despite these challenges, individuals who have experienced sexual trauma often develop strong coping strategies and a heightened sense of self-awareness. You've learned to chart a course in a world that feels inherently unsafe, developing resilience and resourcefulness along the way. However, these same coping mechanisms can also become obstacles. Difficulty with intimacy, self-worth issues, and physical discomfort can make it hard to move forward. It's a delicate dance between protecting yourself and allowing yourself to heal.

Using body scans is highly recommended for sexual trauma. This practice helps you reconnect with your body in a safe and controlled manner. By systematically focusing on different parts of your body, you can start to identify areas of tension and discomfort. Imagine lying down in a quiet room, starting with your toes and slowly working your way up to your head. As you focus on each area, notice any sensations without judgment. This practice can help you develop a sense of body awareness, making it easier to identify and release stored tension.

Touch and self-massage are also indispensable tools for healing from sexual trauma because they help you reclaim a sense of ownership over your physical self. Gently massage your own shoulders or feet, feeling the tension melt away with each touch. This act of self-care sends a powerful message to your body: "I am here. I am safe. I deserve to be taken care of." Self-massage can be particularly favorable for those who struggle with physical touch from others, providing a way to experience nurturing touch in a controlled and safe manner.

Free movement and dance, once again, offer another pathway to healing because these practices allow you to articulate and process complex emotions related to sexual trauma. When you do these practices, make sure to set yourself up in a room you feel safe. Grant yourself permission to move in whatever way feels comfortable or relieving. Each movement becomes a form of letting go, a way to process and let go of the pain. Dance can be particularly liberating, as it encourages you to inhabit your body fully and joyfully, which you may not have been able to experience since your sexual trauma. It's not about performing a perfect dance; it's about allowing your body to communicate and heal in its own way.

These exercises, when practiced regularly, restore your sexual health, which means you can engage in physical intimacy without fear or pain. Better self-esteem fosters a better relationship with yourself and others, making it easier to form and maintain meaningful connections again. An enhanced sense of safety and intimacy allows you to let your guard down, experiencing moments of closeness without the shadow of trauma hanging over you. These practices aim to create a sense of safety and stability, both within yourself and in your interactions with the world.

RELATIONSHIP TRAUMA

Relationship trauma stems from negative or abusive experiences within interpersonal relationships, whether romantic, familial, friendly, or professional. This type of trauma can also be fueled by racial and cultural discrimination, as well as historical and intergenerational trauma. The resulting emotional and psychological harm often colors your perception of yourself and influences how you interact with others in relationships.

Emotionally, relationship trauma often leaves you grappling with mistrust. You might find it hard to believe that anyone has good intentions, always waiting for the other shoe to drop. Fear of abandonment can make you clingy or overly cautious, never fully allowing yourself to relax in a relationship. Emotional volatility becomes a norm, swinging from intense attachment to equally intense detachment.

Low self-esteem is another common issue, as repeated negative experiences erode your sense of self-worth.

Physically, relationship trauma can manifest in stress-related symptoms like headaches and muscle tension. You might find yourself constantly clenching your jaw or experiencing tension in your shoulders. Digestive issues can also arise as your gut responds to emotional stress. It's like your body is crying out for help, mirroring the emotional turmoil you're going through. These physical symptoms can make you feel even more out of control as if your body is rebelling against you.

Behaviorally, relationship trauma makes it difficult to maintain healthy relationships. You might find yourself repeating unhealthy patterns, jumping from one chaotic relationship to another. Fear of intimacy can make you withdraw, pushing people away just when you need them the most. These behaviors create a vicious cycle, where the very actions meant to protect you end up isolating you further. It's like trying to drive with the brakes on—you're not going anywhere fast.

Despite these challenges, you've likely learned to identify patterns and adjust in relationships, a skill that can serve you well on occasion. However, these adaptations can also be barriers. Struggles with trust, emotional regulation, unhealthy attachment, and relationship stability often persist, making it hard to break free from the cycle of trauma.

A movement technique known as postural awareness can be particularly helpful for addressing relationship trauma. Postural awareness in somatic therapy involves recognizing how you hold your body, the impact that posture has on your emotional state, and how you are perceived. For example, slumped shoulders can signal feelings of insecurity or fatigue, while an upright posture can convey confidence and readiness. By tuning into these physical cues, you can gain clarity around your emotions and how they manifest in your body. This awareness not only helps you identify negative patterns but also empowers you to consciously adjust your posture to embody a more positive emotional state. Ultimately, enhancing your postural awareness can lead to improved self-esteem, better communication, and you can start to make conscious changes that reflect your inner growth.

Regulated processing such as pendulation and titration are another way to assist in processing relational trauma since this approach emphasizes bodily sensations to assist you in processing and releasing stored trauma. By paying attention to how your body feels in different relational contexts, you can start to identify and address the underlying issues. Imagine noticing a tightness in your chest when you think about a particular relationship. By focusing on this sensation and allowing it to dissipate, you can start to release the emotional hold it has on you.

Healthier relationships become possible as you learn to trust and set boundaries. Enhanced emotional regulation means you're more prepared to manage relational stress and triggers. Better self-awareness in relational contexts allows you to identify and change unhealthy patterns. These practices aim to create a sense of safety and stability, both within yourself and in your interactions with others.

· · ·

Relationship trauma might have shaped your past, but it doesn't have to define your future. By engaging in somatic practices addressing your unique experiences, you're taking active steps toward healing and growth. Each conscious breath, each mindful movement, and each moment of self-awareness brings you closer to healthier, more fulfilling relationships. So take a moment, breathe deeply, and remember that you have the power to create the relational life you deserve.

INTEGRATING SOMATIC THERAPY WITH OTHER HEALING MODALITIES

"We cannot shame ourselves into change. We can only love ourselves Into evolution."

- UNKNOWN

Have you ever been in a busy train or subway station, and the noise, the people, the constant movement—it's overwhelming? Now, imagine someone hands you a pair of noise-canceling headphones and a map. Suddenly, the chaos feels manageable. This is what integrating somatic therapy with other healing modalities can do for your trauma recovery. It's like adding tools to your emotional toolbox, making the overwhelming feel more manageable. In this chapter, we'll cover how combining somatic therapy with talk therapy can create a synergistic approach to healing.

COMBINING SOMATIC THERAPY WITH TALK THERAPY

Talk therapy, also known as psychotherapy or counseling, is a foundational approach to mental health treatment. It involves examining your thoughts, feelings, and experiences with a trained therapist who helps you understand and manage your mental health challenges. The goal is to achieve more clarity, develop healthy coping strategies, and work through emotional difficulties. Talk therapy comes in various forms, including psychodynamic therapy, humanistic therapy, and cognitive-behavioral therapy. Each approach offers unique improvements, but they all share the common thread of using conversation as a primary tool for healing.

Combining talk therapy with somatic therapy is complementary. Think of talk therapy as a sturdy foundation, providing structure and support. If you were baking a cake, the cake itself represents that foundation, while somatic therapy acts as the frosting, adding layers of depth and richness. Together, they create a more complete, satisfying experience. Integrating these two modalities allows you to address both the cognitive and somatic aspects of trauma, leading to more deep healing.

One of the main benefits of this integration is the ability to enhance emotional processing through bodily awareness to better address the layers of trauma. As we know, trauma often lodges itself in the body, manifesting as physical symptoms like tension, pain, or digestive issues. By mixing somatic techniques with talk therapy sessions, you can tap into these physical experiences and use them as gateways to emotional healing.

· · ·

Let's break down some practical techniques for integrating somatic therapy into traditional talk therapy sessions. You can use body awareness to identify emotional blocks. During a session, you can close your eyes and focus on your body. Where do you feel tightness or discomfort? What sensations arise when you talk about specific experiences? By tuning into these physical cues, you get a clearer understanding of the emotions stored in your body. This awareness can help you and your therapist identify areas that need attention and work through them with more precision.

Breathwork can be instrumental when recalling traumatic memories. Use the specific breathing patterns we touched upon earlier to regulate your nervous system and manage stress. While recounting a difficult memory, you might feel overwhelmed and struggle to stay present. You have the option to begin some breathing exercises to help stabilize your nervous system and keep you grounded. For instance, you could practice diaphragmatic breathing—taking slow, deep breaths from your diaphragm—to activate your body's relaxation response. This can make it easier to process the memory without becoming emotionally flooded.

If you're in a therapy session working through a particularly painful event, you may notice your chest tightening and your breath becoming shallow. Pause for a moment, share what you are feeling with your therapist, and suggest a short grounding exercise. This grounding technique helps you stay present and engaged, allowing you to process the memory more completely.

Another example involves working with your therapist on issues related to anxiety. Whenever you mention a specific trigger, you notice a familiar knot forming in your stomach. You can incorporate progressive muscle relaxation into your session. As you practice this, you become more attuned to the tension in your stomach and learn how to release it. Over time, this practice helps you manage your anxiety better and reduces the physical symptoms associated with it.

This collaborative approach acknowledges the interconnectedness of mind and body, providing you with a better way to deal with the complexities of trauma with more ease and resilience. The combination can also help you develop a more compassionate relationship with your body. Since trauma often leaves us feeling disconnected from our physical selves, sometimes it can feel as if our bodies are betraying us with their symptoms and sensations. This is an invitation to learn to view your body as an ally instead. Shifting your perspective can cultivate a stronger sense of self-acceptance. So, the next time you find yourself overwhelmed by memory or struggling with anxiety, remember that you have a range of tools at your disposal. Embrace these practices with an open mind, and remember that the road to recovery is one that you don't have to face alone.

Reflection Exercise: Exploring Your Somatic Responses

• Find a quiet space where you feel safe and comfortable.

• Close your eyes and take a few deep breaths.

• Reflect on a recent therapy session or a conversation about a challenging experience.

• Notice any physical sensations that arise—tightness, warmth, tingling, or discomfort.

• Mentally note or write down your observations and any emotions associated with these sensations. Share your reflections with your therapist in your next session to try out these somatic responses further.

INTEGRATING SOMATIC PRACTICES WITH COGNITIVE BEHAVIORAL THERAPY (CBT)

Have you ever been in a therapy session, trying to reframe a negative thought about yourself? You logically understand that the thought is irrational, but your body is still tense, your heart is racing, and you feel like you're on the edge of a cliff. This is where integrating somatic practices with Cognitive Behavioral Therapy (CBT) can make a world of difference.

Cognitive Behavioral Therapy, or CBT, is a specific type of talk therapy and a widely used therapeutic approach that focuses on identifying and changing negative thought patterns and behaviors. It's like having a mental resource kit that helps you tackle distorted thinking and replace it with healthier, more grounded thoughts. The primary goal of CBT is cognitive restructuring—altering the way you think to bring about changes in how you feel and behave. The techniques are structured and goal-oriented, often involving homework assignments that reinforce what you discuss during sessions.

The complementary nature of CBT and somatic practices is powerful. While CBT works on reshaping your thoughts, somatic therapy addresses the physical sensations and emotions stored in your body. Consider trying to fix a leaky roof without addressing the water damage inside the house. CBT is like repairing the roof, while somatic therapy helps you clean up and restore the interior. Together, they offer a multi-dimensional approach to healing.

One of the primary ways somatic practices enhance CBT is by bringing bodily awareness into cognitive restructuring. When you're working to change a negative thought, tuning into your body's sensations can provide enlightening realizations into the underlying emotions and beliefs driving your thoughts and behaviors that can help you address the root causes of your distress. For example, you might experience a tightness in your throat when thinking, "I can't communicate my feelings." This physical indicator can reveal underlying emotions that need attention. By addressing both the thought and the bodily sensation, you elevate and enhance your ability to heal.

CBT also involves challenging negative self-talk and replacing it with kinder, more gentle thoughts. However, cognitive work can be mentally exhausting and challenging, especially when you're confronting tightly held and ingrained beliefs. When in a session, working on reframing a thought that has been a part of your identity for years and you challenge this thought, anxiety starts to build, making it hard to think clearly. Somatic techniques help you manage the stress that can arise during CBT exercises. Taking short breaks to move your body can help reset your mind. Taking a few minutes to stretch, walk around, or do a quick body scan can refresh your mind and body. This movement helps release tension, reduce stress, and prepare you for the next cognitive task.

Another practical and instrumental way to combine somatic therapy with CBT is by using grounding techniques before challenging cognitive exercises. Grounding helps anchor you in the present moment, reducing anxiety and creating a sense of stability. This uncomplicated practice can recalibrate your nervous system, leading to a smoother engagement with the mental work ahead.

Breathing exercises are an additional useful tool to integrate with CBT. When you're working on exposure therapy, which involves gradually confronting feared situations or memories, anxiety is almost inevitable. When you feel that anxious or panicky feeling coming on, practicing deep, diaphragmatic breathing can help regulate your nervous system and keep you grounded. This practice can help you stay present and levelheaded, making the exposure process more manageable and productive.

By using methods like movement breaks to refresh your mind and body, grounding techniques to help you stay present, and breathing exercises to regulate your nervous system, you can address the physical manifestations of trauma and work through emotional blocks more effectively. This all-encompassing approach provides multiple pathways for healing and resilience.

COMBINING SOMATIC THERAPY WITH EMDR

Eye Movement Desensitization and Reprocessing (EMDR), which sounds more like a secret agent code than a therapy technique, was developed by Francine Shapiro in the late 1980s. It is a psychotherapeutic approach specifically designed for trauma. It works by using bilateral stimulation techniques—like eye movements, taps/tappers, or auditory tones—to help process and integrate traumatic memories, diminishing the intensity and vividness of the emotions tied to them. The core idea is that trauma disrupts the brain's natural ability to process information properly, and bilateral stimulation helps rewire the brain to resolve these memories.

EMDR therapy typically unfolds in eight phases. The first phase involves taking a detailed history and developing a treatment plan. The next phases focus on preparing you for the process, including teaching you coping strategies and ensuring you have a strong support system. During the assessment phase, you and your therapist identify specific memories to target. It may be productive to first create a trauma timeline and use one of these events. The desensitization phase is where the magic happens: using bilateral stimulation, your therapist guides you through the traumatic memory, helping you reprocess it until it no longer holds the same emotional charge. Subsequent phases focus on installing more flexible beliefs, scanning your body for residual tension, and ensuring that you have a clear plan for moving forward.

Combining EMDR with somatic therapy can enhance the healing process in profound ways. Imagine trying to build a house with just a hammer. Sure, you can get some work done, but add a saw, a drill, and a level, and you're much more equipped. EMDR and somatic therapy together offer a more dynamic solution for trauma recovery. One of the main advantages is the ability to enhance the processing of traumatic memories. While EMDR is more focused on the cognitive and emotional aspects, somatic therapy adds the physical dimension, addressing how trauma is stored in your body. This combination also allows for a deeper healing experience, where mental, emotional, and physical aspects are all addressed.

EMDR can be intense, therefore another significant benefit is the stabilization of the nervous system during sessions. Trauma can leave your nervous system in a state of chaos, oscillating between hyperarousal and hypoarousal. Integrating somatic techniques can help regulate this, making the EMDR process more tolerable and effective. For instance, using grounding techniques beforehand helps create a sense of safety and stability and prepares your nervous system for the upcoming work. Afterward, use grounding techniques to help reorient yourself to the present moment. This might involve focusing on the room around you or drinking a glass of water, focusing on all five senses. Breathwork or engaging in gentle movement helps reorient you in the present moment, transition smoothly out of the session, and integrate the work done.

Body awareness is ideal to use during bilateral stimulation. During the desensitization phase of EMDR, as you focus on the bilateral stimulation and the traumatic memory, pay attention to the physical sensations that arise in your body. Notice any areas of tension, tightness, or discomfort. You may want to try to breathe into these areas, allowing the sensations to shift and release. This body awareness can provide fresh perspectives into how trauma is stored in your body and help facilitate its release. For example, if you notice tightness in your chest while processing a memory, taking deep breaths and focusing on relaxing that area can help dissolve the tension.

Another technique for integrating somatic therapy with EMDR is using somatic resources during the installation phase. After desensitizing the traumatic memory, the installation phase focuses on strengthening more adaptive beliefs and positive emotions. Using somatic resources—such as visualizing a safe place or recalling a positive memory—can enhance this process. Imagine you've just processed a difficult memory, and now you're focusing on a new, empowering belief. As you visualize this belief, notice how it feels in your body. Where do you feel warmth or lightness? By tuning into these positive sensations and amplifying them, you can reinforce the new belief on a deeper level.

Using somatic techniques like gentle touch can also help manage any residual tension or discomfort that emerges during EMDR sessions. Additionally, after an EMDR session, take a few moments to scan your body from head to toe, noticing any areas that still feel tense or uncomfortable. Your therapist might guide you to breathe into these areas or use gentle touch to help release the tension. This practice helps ensure that any lingering physical manifestations of trauma are addressed, promoting a more thorough and integrated healing process.

If you are in an EMDR session, processing a memory that brings up feelings of shame and self-blame. As the bilateral stimulation continues, you notice a heavy feeling in your chest. Experiment with placing your hand on your chest and offer yourself compassionate words, like "It's okay; you're safe now." This somatic practice helps you connect with your body in a supportive way, reinforcing the healing work of the EMDR session.

Combining EMDR with somatic therapy provides support and acts like a life vest when you need it most. These approaches help anchor you in the present moment, reducing the risk of becoming overwhelmed by traumatic memories. By addressing the cognitive, emotional, and physical dimensions of trauma, you can achieve a more integrated healing experience. Techniques such as grounding, body awareness, and somatic resourcing enhance the effectiveness of EMDR, making the process more manageable and thorough.

USING TECHNOLOGY TO ENHANCE SOMATIC PRACTICES

There are a variety of digital tools and devices available to you that can enhance your somatic practices. These technological advancements open up new ways to connect and engage with your body and emotions, offering valuable insights and support. The inclusion of these tools is not an endorsement. Instead, they are additional options to improve your practice and make it more accessible to support your success. Please note that while this technology exists at the time of publishing, it evolves rapidly—new products may emerge, and some may become obsolete, along with the information about these tools. So, be sure to check their current availability and see which best suits your needs. Please refer to the resources sheet at the end of this book for more information on how to access all the tools mentioned in this chapter.

The following apps are fantastic tools to boost your somatic practice. They offer a range of exercises customized to different schedules: quick exercises for those busy moments and longer sessions for when you have more time to unwind. Many blend mindfulness elements alongside somatic components, inviting you to really tune into your body and emotions. You'll find practices like breathwork, body scans, gentle movement, and mindfulness activities, all aimed at managing stress and anxiety and improving body awareness and emotional regulation. They guide you through different techniques, providing visual and auditory cues. It's like having a personal coach in your pocket. There's something here for everyone, helping you discover the techniques that resonate most with you. The beauty of these apps lies in their accessibility—you can use them anytime, anywhere, making it easier to integrate somatic practices into your daily routine.

• **SomaShare**: A community-driven platform connecting users to somatic practices and peer support for emotional and physical well-being.

• **Embodymind**: This app offers guided somatic practices designed to enhance body awareness and mindfulness.

• **NEUROFIT**: Focuses on neurophysiological practices aimed at improving body awareness, relaxation, and emotional resilience.

• **Somawell**: Provides tools and techniques for enhancing well-being through somatic practices and mindfulness.

• **SomaIQ**: This app offers a variety of somatic exercises and resources to deepen body awareness and emotional processing.

• **Breathe2Relax**: A guided breathing app designed to help you manage stress and anxiety, fostering relaxation and emotional balance.

• **Othership**: A guided breathwork app that combines somatic techniques with mindfulness practices for emotional regulation.

• **Insight Timer**: Features a vast library of guided meditations and mindfulness practices that support somatic awareness.

• **Headspace**: Offers guided meditations and practices focused on enhancing body awareness and emotional well-being. Also, offer exercises for kids.

• **Calm**: Includes mindfulness exercises, breathing techniques, and body scans to promote relaxation and somatic practices.

• **Smiling Mind**: A mindfulness app with programs designed for different age groups, promoting emotional well-being and body awareness. Also, offer exercises for kids.

• **Day One:** A journaling app designed to help you document your thoughts and experiences, promoting self-reflection and emotional processing. Though not specifically for somatic therapy, it includes prompts, mood tracking, multimedia entries, customizable templates, and habit trackers, which would all be especially helpful in supporting your somatic practice.

Wearable devices can also enhance your somatic practices by providing real-time feedback on your body's responses. Heart rate variability monitors, for instance, measure the variations in time between your heartbeats, offering a glimpse into your nervous system's health. You can likely use those built into your smartwatch or smart ring or download separate apps with more tracking features, which can also monitor your activity levels and sleep patterns. This can help you identify how your daily habits impact your well-being. Experiment with devices that alert you when your stress levels are rising, prompting you to take a moment to breathe and recalibrate. However, that is not fitting for everyone; some may find this distracting or stressful which would defeat the purpose, so do what works best for you.

Virtual reality (VR) is another exciting frontier for somatic therapy. VR-based guided visualizations offer immersive experiences that can help you connect with your body and emotions in new ways. Using VR for a wide range of therapy, including somatic therapy, is a relatively new concept with growing applications. Putting on a VR headset is like being transported right onto the sand of a serene beach or the grassy top of a majestic mountain, where you can practice guided visualizations in a safe and soothing environment. VR can also create virtual safe spaces, providing a sense of security and comfort as you engage with your own somatic practices. These immersive experiences can enhance the effectiveness of somatic therapy, offering new ways to examine and process your emotions. Of all of the tools discussed in this chapter, these devices are on the higher end of the price spectrum. So, if you have one already available to you (or can borrow from your kid), then this is a really fun option to use. That said, I wouldn't necessarily recommend running out to get one just to encourage your somatic practice. Listed below are a few of the mindfulness apps currently available that can help create a virtual, serene environment when you don't have physical access to one or just want to switch things up.

. . .

- **TRIPP**: For Meta Quest - A mindfulness and meditation app designed for immersive experiences.

- **Guided Meditation VR**: Guided Meditation VR on Steam - Features a variety of guided meditations in immersive 3D environments.

- **Nature Treks VR**: Nature Treks VR on Steam - Offers a serene space for mindfulness and relaxation exercises through exploration.

Online guided somatic exercises are another valuable resource. YouTube is one of the best places to find a wide range of on-demand guided somatic practices. The bonus is most are free. Guided practices provide clear instructions and a sense of direction, making it easier to engage with somatic techniques. Following along with a video can guide you through breathing techniques to settle your nerves or gentle movement sequences to help you release tension and connect with your body while you listen and follow along. These resources can be a lifeline, offering extra guidance and support when you need it. Please see the key search terms in the reference guide. You can store and organize the videos in your account, making it easy to access when you wake up or go to bed.

Incorporating technology into your somatic therapy practices and into your daily routine can be a game-changer! It offers numerous benefits, from increased accessibility and convenience to real-time feedback and immersive experiences. Digital tools like these apps provide added support, making it easier to engage with somatic techniques. Wearable devices provide metrics about your body's responses, helping you track your progress and adjust your practices as needed. Virtual reality opens up new possibilities for immersive and safe somatic experiences by integrating these technological tools. Setting reminders or app notifications for practice sessions can help you stay consistent and committed to your somatic practices. These reminders can serve as cues to pause, breathe, and reconnect with your body, making it easier to incorporate somatic practices into your busy schedule. However, it's important to use technology mindfully. While apps and devices offer beneficial support and can enhance your somatic practices, it's easy to become over-reliant on them. Ensuring that technology serves as a tool rather than a distraction or a crutch is integral. Take breaks from screens when needed, and make sure to engage in somatic practices without technological aids from time to time, allowing your own awareness to guide you. This approach balances technology and mindfulness, focusing on internal guidance rather than external instruction.

PRACTICAL APPLICATIONS FOR EVERYDAY LIFE & MAKING IT WORK FOR YOU

"The best practice is the one you actually do"

- MICHAELA BOEHM

This chapter is all about bringing somatic practices into your daily routine. Life can be hectic, and the thought of adding new techniques might feel overwhelming. Rest assured—this chapter is designed to show you just how easily you can customize and weave these practices into your busy life. You'll discover how to use somatic markers for more intuitive decision-making and find techniques fitting your unique needs for managing stress and improving sleep. On top of that, we will cover different micro-practices that seamlessly fit into even the tightest schedules. Then, we'll bring everything together into an action plan, showing you how to establish a daily practice that feels "doable," rewarding, and sustainable. This is about making small, meaningful changes with lasting results to feel grounded and more connected to yourself than ever before.

USING SOMATIC MARKERS FOR DECISION MAKING

Think about the last time you made a tough decision. Did you get a sinking feeling in your stomach? Or maybe your heart raced, and your palms got sweaty. These physical sensations are known as somatic markers. They are your body's way of signaling an emotional response to a particular situation, basically guiding you towards or away from certain choices. For example, a tight chest might indicate anxiety, while a relaxed, open posture could signal comfort and readiness. Developed by neuroscientist Antonio Damasio, the Somatic Marker Hypothesis suggests that these bodily signals play a vital role in decision-making. When you experience an emotional trigger, your body sends out these alerts, letting you know something requires your attention and assisting you in addressing the situation. By paying attention to your body's signals, you can make choices that align with your authentic self. This leads to greater emotional regulation, as you're less likely to be swayed by external pressures or internal anxieties. When your decisions come from a place of bodily awareness, they are more likely to reflect your core beliefs and desires, helping you stay true to your personal values.

Additionally, after you notice and recognize these sensations, you can use somatic practices to interrupt the pattern and regulate your nervous system, restoring steadiness. Good old grounding and breathwork can come in handy here as well. You can also use gentle movement to help release residual tension or try stretching or taking a short walk to reconnect with your body. By interpreting your body's signals, you can make more informed and intuitive decisions, and using somatic practices to bring yourself back to baseline helps create new neural pathways, making it easier to manage emotional triggers in the future.

. . .

Reflection Exercise: Discovering Somatic Markers

- Think about a recent decision you made. What physical sensations did you notice in your body? Did your stomach churn when you made a particular choice? Did your shoulders tense up? These are your unique somatic markers.
- How did these sensations influence your choice?
- Reflect on a time when you ignored your body's signals.
- What was the outcome?

Writing down your experiences and noting any recurring sensations can be incredibly helpful for uncovering patterns. Over time, you'll start to see connections between certain feelings and your body's responses.

To practice using somatic markers in decision-making, start with small choices. Notice your gut reactions during everyday decisions, like what to eat for lunch or what to wear. Tune into your body and see what it tells you. Role-playing scenarios can also be revealing. For instance, imagine choosing a new job. Pay attention to your body's cues as you think about taking the job or not. Does one choice make you feel more relaxed and open, while the other causes tension? Try to notice the nuances and use the signals to guide your decision. That tension around new experiences can stem from doubt or fear, but it doesn't necessarily mean you should shy away from them. This discomfort often arises from stepping outside your comfort zone, so explore where those feelings are coming from and consider whether they're holding you back from exciting opportunities. However, if your gut instinct signals that something doesn't align with your values or needs, that's a different kind of unease worth listening to. By distinguishing between the two, you can assess your choices more wisely, embracing growth while honoring your intuition.

.   .   .

After experiencing an emotional trigger or crisis, post-trigger recovery practices are crucial for regaining a sense of harmony. Reflecting on your bodily sensations can also provide enlightening discoveries about how the trigger affected you. You may want to write down what you felt and how you responded. This reflection can inform future decisions and help you better understand your somatic markers. Additionally, self-soothing touch practices, like placing a hand on your heart or gently massaging your temples, can provide comfort and relaxation.

Using somatic markers for decision-making is like having an internal GPS guiding you toward choices that align with your true self. By tuning into your body's signals and responding with somatic practices, you can handle life's challenges with more ease and confidence. Your body holds immense wisdom, and by listening to it, you can make more intuitive choices that better fit your intrinsic values and aspirations.

USING SOMATIC TECHNIQUES TO MANAGE STRESS AT HOME & WORK

You're sitting at your desk, or maybe even your kitchen table these days, buried under a pile of proverbial paperwork or maybe piles of endless laundry, and your shoulders feel like they're made of concrete. Your jaw is clenched, and you haven't taken a deep breath in what feels like hours. Sound familiar? Household and work-related stress is a common culprit behind physical tension and emotional strain. For people who have experienced trauma, the pressure and expectations in these everyday situations can be particularly intense and overwhelming. You may find that ordinary stressors trigger more severe reactions, as your nervous systems are often more sensitive to perceived "threats." Physical tension often shows up as tight shoulders, a stiff neck, or a clenched jaw. Emotional triggers at work might include looming deadlines, challenging colleagues, or an over-whelming workload. Likewise, at home, your emotional triggers may be parent-related and stem from endless to-do lists, managing kids' moods, or feeling overwhelmed by unrelenting household responsibilities. These triggers activate your body's stress response, leading to increased heart rate, shallow breathing, and muscle tension. By identifying these signs, you can intervene with somatic techniques to manage your stress before it takes a toll on your well-being.

When stress strikes, using a quick grounding exercise can help you regain your footing. Specifically, the 5-4-3-2-1 method covered in chapter four, where you identify five things you can see, four things you can touch, three things you can hear, two things you can smell, and one thing you can taste. This engages your senses and anchors you in the present moment. You can try box breathing as well. Repeat this cycle a few times to compose yourself. Don't forget that stretches or "shaking it out" can also release physical tension. Stretch your arms overhead, roll your shoulders, shake out your hands, and gently tilt your head from side to side. These easy movements can break the cycle of stress and bring relief quickly.

Managing long-term stress requires a proactive approach. Set reminders on your phone or use an app to take intermittent breaks for movement and breathwork every hour. These mini-breaks can prevent tension buildup and keep your energy levels steady. Recognizing physical tension and emotional triggers is the first step to mitigating stress and keeping overwhelmed at bay. By incorporating these immediate relief techniques and regular breaks into your routine, you can stay centered and focused throughout the day."

SOMATIC PRACTICES FOR IMPROVED SLEEP

The toll trauma takes on sleep can feel like a never-ending nightmare. Have you ever laid awake at 3 a.m., staring at the ceiling, your mind replaying the worst moments of your life on repeat? Trauma can wreak havoc on your sleep patterns, leading to chronic insomnia and restless nights. The link between trauma and insomnia is well-documented. Trauma often keeps your nervous system in a state of hyperarousal, making it difficult to relax and fall asleep. Somatic symptoms like muscle tension, a racing heart, and shallow breathing can disrupt your sleep, leaving you exhausted and irritable the next day. This is where somatic practices become exceptionally valuable—they help soothe your body and mind, creating a conducive environment for restful sleep.

Establishing a pre-sleep somatic routine can be revolutionary to induce better sleep. Start with gentle stretching or self-massage before bed. This can help release physical tension and prepare your body for rest. Focus on areas where you typically hold stress, like your shoulders, neck, and lower back. Simple stretches, like reaching for your toes or gently twisting your torso, can make a big difference. Next, try progressive muscle relaxation (PMR). Lie down in a comfortable position and slowly tense and then release each muscle group, starting from your toes and working up to your head to ease muscle tension and signal to your body that it's time to relax.

Visualization can also be a great compliment to your pre-sleep routine. Picture a serene, safe space—perhaps a tranquil lake or a cozy cabin in the woods. Close your eyes and immerse yourself in this scene, engaging all your senses. Imagine the sound of the waves, the smell of the ocean, or the warmth of the sun on your skin. This mental escape can help quiet your mind and create a sense of safety, making it easier to drift off to sleep.

Not being able to get to sleep is rough, but waking up in the middle of the night can be incredibly frustrating, especially when it feels impossible to fall back asleep. If you find yourself in this situation, grounding techniques can help you return to sleep. Try focusing on the sensation of your body against the mattress. Notice the weight of your blanket and the texture of your sheets. This can help anchor you in the present moment and reduce anxiety. Breathing exercises can also be advantageous. Practice deep, slow breaths, inhaling through your nose and exhaling through your mouth. This can activate your parasympathetic nervous system, helping you fall back asleep.

In addition to daily somatic practices, try getting some morning sunlight exposure to support your overall sleep quality. Sunlight helps regulate your circadian rhythm, signaling to your body when it's time to be awake and when it's time to sleep. Spend some time outside in the morning, even if it's just for a few minutes, if you can. Routine physical activity is also highly recommended. Exercise helps reduce stress and anxiety, making it easier to fall and stay asleep. Aim for at least 30 minutes of moderate exercise most days of the week, but try to avoid any vigorous activity within a few hours before bedtime.

Evening somatic practices can be a wonderful addition to your sleep routine and a soothing way to wind down before sleep. Set aside some quiet time in the evening. Begin by finding a quiet space where you feel comfortable, preferably in your bedroom on your bed. Lie down on your back with your knees bent and feet flat on the floor or the bed. Take a few deep breaths, allowing your body to relax into the ground. As you breathe in, visualize drawing in solace, and as you exhale, imagine releasing any tension or stress. Gently bring your awareness to different parts of your body, starting from your toes and moving up to your head, noticing any sensations or areas of tightness. Spend a few moments simply being with these feelings, allowing them to soften. This practice can help you connect with your body and result in a greater sense of tranquility, making it easier for you to drift off into a restful sleep without a million things still running around your mind.

Although trauma's grip on sleep can be pervasive, somatic practices offer a powerful way to reclaim your nights. By incorporating a pre-sleep routine with gentle stretching, progressive muscle relaxation, and visualization, you can create an environment conducive to rest. Middle-of-the-night practices like grounding techniques and breathing exercises can help you return to sleep when disruptions occur. Daily somatic practices can improve overall sleep quality to wake up feeling more refreshed, resilient, and ready to face each new day.

MICRO-PRACTICES FOR BUSY LIVES

The concept of micro-practices is groundbreaking for anyone feeling overwhelmed by the idea of adding yet another task to their already packed schedule. These are short, focused practices specifically designed for those with limited time. Think of them as the espresso shots of somatic therapy—quick, potent, and effective. The charm of micro-practices is their simplicity and accessibility. You don't need a special setting or a large chunk of free time to benefit from them. Even a few minutes of intentional practice can add up to significant gains over time. Just as a plane adjusting its course by one degree can reach its intended destination, these small, consistent practices can guide you toward remarkable transformations. Each micro-practice acts like a subtle course correction, steering you towards greater emotional balance and resilience. Over time, these micro-practices accumulate, creating a reservoir of stability and peacefulness that you can draw from whenever you need it. They help you stay anchored, present, and connected to your body, even amidst the chaos of daily life.

Do you remember one of the micro-practices we covered earlier? It's also one of the simplest techniques—the five-minute body scan. However, you could do a quicker version in one to two minutes if you need to. Find a quiet spot, close your eyes, and slowly bring your attention to different parts of your body, starting from your toes and moving up to your head. Notice any sensations without judgment. This practice helps you quickly tune into your body and release any tension you might be holding.

Another micro-practice you can perform is a short grounding technique. Let's do a quick refresher. Take a moment to feel your feet firmly planted on the ground. Wiggle your toes and notice the texture of the floor beneath you. Notice the sensations in your body, and take a few deep breaths. You can easily do this discretely whenever you are waiting in line, especially if you start getting impatient while waiting. This turns an otherwise idle moment into an opportunity for self-care. This small act of grounding can help you feel more stable and present, especially during stressful moments. It's like hitting the reset button on your nervous system, helping you shift gears smoothly and maintain a sense of ease throughout the day.

Brief, mindful breathing exercises are also incredibly useful. Try this: inhale deeply through your nose for a count of four, hold for a count of four, and exhale through your mouth for a count of four. Repeat this cycle a few times, focusing on the sensation of your breath. Do you recall what this one is called? Box breathing. It activates the parasympathetic nervous system, promoting peacefulness and reducing anxiety. It's a fast and easy way to steady your mind and body, no matter where you are. Incorporating micro-practices into your daily routines is easier than you might think. Try this short exercise.

Action Item: Identifying Micro-practice Opportunities

Take a quick moment right now to start identifying moments in your day where you can slip in a brief practice.

• How about a mini body scan during a work break or every time you have to refill your water bottle?

• Instead of scrolling through your phone, could you take those few minutes to tune into your body? Notice any areas of tension and consciously relax them. This little check-in can refresh your mind and body, making you more productive and focused.

• How about your morning or evening routines? Can you start your day with a brief mindful breathing exercise to establish an even tone, or end your day with a five-minute body scan to release the day's stress and prepare for restful sleep?

• What transitions do you usually encounter on a daily basis when you are moving from one task to another? Maybe when you get in the car to drive to work, or the gym, or maybe before or after school, pick up and drop off. (Obviously not while driving).

• Focus on finding pockets of time where you can easily incorporate these practices without feeling like you're adding more to your plate. Using these moments as cues and reminders will naturally encourage consistency.

. . .

The flexibility and simplicity of micro-practices make them a perfect fit for busy lives. They allow you to stay connected to your body and manage stress, even when time is limited. By making these small but impactful practices a part of your daily routine, you create a foundation of resilience to support you. Somatic exercises serve as your daily workout for the nervous system, like a running routine that keeps your lungs healthy. These exercises help maintain emotional balance and prevent your nerves from going haywire. Micro-practices, on the other hand, are like inhalers. They can be used regularly and provide quick relief in stressful moments, offering instant support when you need it. Imagine building a fortress of emotional strength, brick by brick. That's what you're doing when you incorporate these small but powerful practices into your daily life. These micro-practices are like little gifts you give yourself throughout the day, each one a reminder that you deserve care and attention, no matter how busy life gets. So go ahead, take those five minutes—you're worth it!

TAILORING PRACTICES TO INDIVIDUAL NEEDS

Have you ever tried on a one-size-fits-all outfit? It's often too tight in some places, too loose in others, and just plain uncomfortable. The same goes for somatic practices. Different trauma responses require different approaches, so tailoring these practices to individual experiences and needs increases your engagement and therapeutic value. By customizing your somatic exercises, you can address the unique ways trauma manifests in your life, making the process more meaningful.

In order to start customizing your practices, it's helpful to identify and assess your personal triggers and preferences. Take note of the situations, people, or environments that tend to trigger your trauma responses. Pay attention to how your body reacts—do you feel tightness in your chest, a lump in your throat, or a knot in your stomach? Identifying these triggers and corresponding physical sensations can guide you in choosing the most suitable somatic techniques. Additionally, consider your personal preferences. Do you find movement more soothing than stillness? Does deep breathing help you relax, or do you prefer grounding exercises? Your comfort level with different practices is a key factor in how well they work for you."

Once you've identified your triggers and preferences, modify techniques based on feedback and comfort levels. If a particular practice feels overwhelming or ineffective, tweak it to better suit your needs. For instance, if a full-body scan feels too intense, try focusing on just one or two areas of your body. If deep breathing makes you dizzy, experiment with shorter, more frequent breaths. Combining various practices addresses multiple aspects of your trauma. To find what works best for you, experiment with different techniques periodically to see how they feel, and update and change as you see fit. Keep an open mind and be patient with the process. Please know that what works today might not work tomorrow, and that's okay. The goal is to build a collection of practices that you can draw from as needed. Noting what feels most favorable can guide you in refining your routine. Consider keeping a journal to track your experiences, noting which practices bring the most and least relief. Over time, you'll develop a richer understanding of your body's needs and signals.

Tailoring somatic practices to your personal needs is like composing a song for your unique rhythm. By assessing personal triggers and preferences, modifying techniques based on feedback, and combining various practices, you can create a well-rounded approach to healing. Encouraging self-exploration and noting what feels most beneficial ensures that your routine remains dynamic and gets you the best results.

DEVELOPING A DAILY SOMATIC PRACTICE

It is finally time to bring all the concepts together and start crafting your personalized action plan. Creating a somatic practice is like planting a garden with the digging, planting, and watering—but over time, you see the fruits of your labor. Making somatic practices a natural part of daily life reduces the feeling of extra work and integrates healing into your routine. This also provides long-term benefits, gradually reducing trauma symptoms and expanding your emotional capacity. Over time, as you repeat these actions, they can become habits, or better yet- automatic behaviors that require less conscious thought, helping us do things effortlessly without thinking.

Designing Your Practice

To design a daily somatic practice routine that works best for you, start by assessing your individual needs and preferences. Ask yourself the following questions to get a better idea of how you want to structure your practice:

• What areas of your life need the most support? • What are your goals, and WHY is healing important to you specifically? (Be realistic and focus your energy on growth in the areas that matter most to you.)

• Which trauma type(s) do you identify with most? (You may find it helpful to refer to the suggested practices for that associated trauma.)

• What symptoms do you struggle with most: anxiety, stress, chronic pain, or emotional regulation?

• What is the best time of day for your practice? Some people find mornings to be the most effective, while others prefer evenings. Customize your routine to fit your lifestyle.

•   •   •

Everyone's needs and preferences are different, so it's incredibly important to design a practice that fits seamlessly into your life. For those with limited mobility, modifying practices to fit your capabilities ensures accessibility and progress. Set aside dedicated time somewhere each day for your somatic practices. Find a time that feels right for you and stick to it. It is also a good idea to start small and gradually build on your practice. Consistency is more important than the duration of each practice. Focus on doing what you can. Even a few minutes a day can make a substantial difference over time.

Variety is the spice of life, and the same goes for your somatic practice. Keeping it engaging prevents it from becoming a chore. Rotate different exercises based on your emotional state and mood. Some days, you might need grounding techniques; other days, breathwork might be more helpful. It's all about balancing the different types of exercises. Creating a structured schedule helps maintain consistency. Use reminders to prompt your practices. You can set phone alarms for practice times or place visual cues like post-it notes or objects around your house to remind you.

Sample Practices:

10-minute daily routine: A quick body scan, a few grounding exercises of your choice, and a brief mindful breathing session.

30-minute comprehensive routine: Engage in some gentle movement, progressive muscle relaxation, titration or pendulation, and a visualization that feels best to you.

Bedtime routine: Focus on gentle stretching, progressive muscle relaxation, and visualizing a tranquil, safe space to wind down and quiet the mind and body to prepare for restful sleep.

Morning routine: Start with a body scan, then some breathwork and a little gentle movement or dance to set a positive tone for the day.

Midday routines include a body scan or some progressive muscle relaxation, especially if you have been sitting at a computer most of the day, then a visualization exercise, and finish with gentle movement like shaking it out or breathing exercises for a reset during lunch breaks.

Weekly routine: Choose a day that works best to set aside time for more targeted practices that may involve taking more time or require a safe and quiet space where you won't be bothered to do some longer visualizations, titration, pendulation, or somatic dance, and finish with some grounding and or breathwork.

If you would like an alternative to creating a stand-alone practice, you also have the option to tap into routines you already have. James Clear, in his book *Atomic Habits*, describes this concept as "habit stacking," which is pairing a new habit you want to create, in this case, a somatic practice, with an existing routine. Once these small practices are integrated into your new routine, you can layer in more enriching practices, creating more detailed routines when they are manageable.

By developing a consistent daily somatic practice, you create a sustainable approach to healing that nurtures resilience, emotional stability, and long-term health. Designing a routine that fits your specific needs, incorporating variety, and setting realistic goals ensures your practice grows with you and continues to be engaging.

CONTINUED HEALING AND PERSONAL GROWTH

"Life is too short, or too long, for me to allow myself the luxury of living it so badly."

— PAULO COELHO

In staying with the garden theme- imagine you're a gardener. You've just planted a beautiful array of flowers, but you know the work doesn't stop there. You need to water them, give them sunlight, and occasionally prune them to ensure they thrive. Healing from trauma is a bit like tending to a garden. The initial planting—starting your somatic practice—is just the beginning. To see those flowers bloom, you need to keep nurturing them.

SUSTAINING YOUR SOMATIC PRACTICE OVER TIME

The importance of consistency in maintaining a somatic practice cannot be overstated. Just as a garden needs usual care to flourish, your body and mind require ongoing attention to heal and grow. Consistency in your somatic practices helps prevent the regression of trauma symptoms. When you engage in these practices regularly, you build that strong mind-body connection that has been emphasized frequently. Doing so creates a strong foundation; without it, the structure would be unstable and prone to collapse under stress.

Healing is a continuous process. It's not a straight path but rather a winding journey with ups and downs. There will be days when you feel like you're making great strides and days when you feel like you're back at square one. That's entirely normal. Keep showing up for yourself. By maintaining somatic practices, you create a sense of stability and resilience that carries you through tough times. Consider it a trusty umbrella on a rainy day—while it doesn't stop the rain, it keeps you dry and makes the storm more bearable.

Setting realistic milestones is a fundamental part of keeping your motivation high and your progress on track. Staying motivated can be tough, especially when progress feels slow or stagnant. One way to stay committed is by setting achievable goals. Break down your long-term objectives into smaller, manageable ones. Start with short-term goals that are achievable within a few weeks, such as reducing anxiety during specific situations or improving sleep quality. These goals should be specific and measurable, making it easier to track your progress. For example, a short-term goal could be, "Practice grounding/breathing/somatic movement/PRM exercises daily for two weeks and note any changes in anxiety levels, sleep quality, or emotional stability on a scale from 1 to 10." Over time, these assessments can reveal trends and highlight areas that require more focus. Long-term goals might include more substantial achievements like "Consistently manage stress through breathwork and titration over six months." Ultimately, while setting realistic goals and expectations is a must, it's just as imperative to focus on the practice itself rather than just the outcome. When you commit to the process consistently, you'll often find that the results take care of themselves. This shift in perspective can help alleviate any unnecessary pressure you put on yourself.

Be sure to balance the intensity and frequency of your practices. Start with small, manageable sessions and gradually increase the duration and intensity as you become more comfortable. This approach helps prevent burnout and makes it easier to maintain your routine in the long run. It's like training for a marathon; you wouldn't start by running 26 miles on the first day. You'd begin with shorter distances and slowly build up your endurance. The same principle applies to somatic practices.

Embracing change and listening to your body is an integral part of sustaining your somatic practice over time. As you grow and evolve, your needs and preferences may shift. So, modify your practices to adjust accordingly. If a particular technique no longer feels good, don't be afraid to try something new. For instance, on any given day, you might find certain movements more challenging. In such cases, opt for a gentler method that still provides rewarding improvement without causing strain. Similarly, during particularly stressful periods, you might need to increase the frequency of your exercises to manage heightened anxiety. Aim to find what suits you best in the present moment.

· · ·

Life is unpredictable, and your somatic practice routine should be flexible enough to adjust to its ever-changing nature. There will inevitably be times when your schedule becomes hectic, making it challenging to maintain your usual routine. During such periods, remember to prioritize your mental and emotional well-being while adapting your practice to fit your current circumstances. If you can't commit to your full practice, opt for shorter, more frequent sessions. Remember, something is always better than nothing, and this flexibility ensures that you continue to reap the rewards from your somatic practices, even during busy or stressful times. Flexibility and adaptability are not just short-term solutions but necessary components for long-term success. Your routine should reflect life's unpredictability by allowing for adjustments in exercise intensity and duration based on your current needs. As you progress, introducing new techniques can help keep your practice fresh and enjoyable. Starting with small, manageable steps lays a strong foundation for growth, ensuring that your somatic practice remains a source of support rather than a burden.

It's also helpful to find ways to make your somatic practices enjoyable. Incorporate elements that bring you joy and serenity. This could be playing your favorite music during a movement exercise, practicing breathwork in a serene outdoor setting, or using essential oils during a body scan. When you look forward to your practices, it becomes easier to stay consistent.

Let's not forget the power of community in sustaining your practice. Connecting with others who are also on a healing path can provide much-needed support and encouragement. Join local or online groups focused on somatic practices. Share your experiences, learn from others, and celebrate each other's progress. Being part of a supportive community can make a considerable difference in your motivation and commitment.

As you continue your somatic practice, remember that progress is not always linear. There will be plateaus and setbacks, but these are natural parts of the healing process. It's important to stick with the process, even when progress seems slow. When you encounter a plateau, it's an opportunity to reassess and adjust your practices. Sometimes, trying a new technique or seeking guidance from a professional can help reignite your progress. Stay patient and supportive of yourself. Healing takes time, and every step forward, no matter how small, is a victory.

Remember, sustaining your somatic practice is not about perfection. It's about showing up for yourself consistently and making adjustments as needed to support you through life's challenges. Another wise thing James Clear says is, "You do not rise to the level of your goals. You fall to the level of your systems." By maintaining your practice and creating supportive systems, you nurture your mind and body, allowing them to heal and grow. You're not just surviving; you're thriving. And that is something worth celebrating.

MEASURING PROGRESS AND CELEBRATING SUCCESSES

Regular self-assessments and reflections are invaluable for gauging your progress and reinforcing your commitment to healing. By creating a system that works for you—whether it's a weekly check-in or a monthly review—you can proficiently track your journey. Keeping a somatic practice healing journal is a really great way to do this; it serves as your personal record of growth, where you can document your practices, note the sensations you experienced, and reflect on your emotional state. This process of reflecting and documenting helps solidify your experiences and makes it easier to track patterns over time. Acknowledging your progress in this way not only highlights how far you've come but also helps you identify what methods are optimal for you. Try using templates like the ones below to guide your reflections and see how your practices influence your well-being and where adjustments might be needed. (*Please find BONUS tracking and prompt worksheets in the Somatic Therapy Resources at the back of this book.*)

Self-Assessment Tracker and Reflection Prompts

• Daily Reflection Template (for insight): [example] "Today's practice [included grounding exercises and breathwork]...., I noticed [a sense of calm wash over me]..., I felt [tension release from my shoulders]..."

• Checklist Template (for tracking exercises): [example] "Grounding exercise ✔, Breathwork ✔, Visualization ✔"

• Progress Tracker: [example] "Week 1: I noticed [reduced anxiety] ..., Week 2: I experienced [improved sleep patterns] ..."

Monthly reflection exercises can help you take a step back and evaluate how your practices have impacted your life. These reflections can guide you in fine-tuning your routine to better meet your needs. Self-assessment questionnaires can offer a structured way to evaluate your progress.

Monthly Reflection Exercise

• Reflect on the past month: "What changes have I noticed in my body and emotions?"

• Evaluate effectiveness: "Which practices have been most effective, and why?"

• Identify areas for improvement: "What needs more focus in my practice?"

Noticing your ability to recover from setbacks and maintain more emotional regularity is another critical aspect of tracking progress. Pay attention to how quickly you bounce back from stressful situations. Are you able to ground yourself more easily? Do you find it easier to manage anxiety? These are signs that your somatic practices are working. Identify patterns and triggers that might be causing setbacks. Monitoring these can reveal what needs more attention in your practice. For instance, you might notice that certain triggers consistently disrupt your progress, indicating a need for focused work in those areas.

Celebrating each milestone and achievement, no matter how small, is HUGE for maintaining motivation because it is about acknowledging and honoring your hard work and progress. This could be something like when you feel a sense of contentedness, when you notice reduced anxiety, or when you successfully cope with a trigger. Take time to recognize the effort you've put in and the strides you've made. Reward yourself in ways that support your goals and well-being. This could be as little as writing a congratulatory note to yourself or sharing your success with a close friend or therapist. Letting others you trust know about your progress can provide additional motivation and create a sense of accountability. These celebrations reinforce positive behavior and can amplify your sense of achievement, keeping you motivated to continue your practices. They serve as reminders that even small steps forward are steps in the right direction. It's like having a cheering squad that celebrates your victories with you, making the journey feel less solitary and more supported. If you are feeling creative, you can even make a visual representation of your progress, which can also be incredibly motivating. Consider making a progress chart or timeline that highlights big milestones and achievements. This visual aid serves as a tangible reminder of how far you've come and the progress you've made. It's like having a map that shows the distance you've traveled, reinforcing the idea that you are moving forward, even when it doesn't always feel like it.

Once again, apps and tools can also be beneficial in tracking your progress. There are numerous apps designed to help you log your practices, track your emotional state, and even remind you to engage in your somatic exercises. These digital aids can be particularly useful for those who prefer a structured, tech-savvy approach to tracking. They offer the convenience of having all your data in one place, making it easier to see trends and patterns over time. Whether you prefer a handwritten journal or a digital tracker, what truly matters is trying to document your experience consistently.

As you continue to track and reflect on your progress, remember that healing is a dynamic process with natural ebbs and flows. There will be times when you feel you're making big strides and times when progress seems slow or stagnant. Stay committed and keep moving forward. By regularly measuring your progress, setting attainable goals, and celebrating your achievements, you create a positive feedback loop. Ultimately, this process is about building a deeper connection with yourself and recognizing the effort you've invested, the challenges you've overcome, and the growth you've achieved.

OVERCOMING PLATEAUS AND SETBACKS IN YOUR HEALING JOURNEY

Recognizing plateaus in your healing journey can feel like hitting a wall. You've been making progress, and then suddenly, everything seems to stall. Stagnation in emotional or physical progress is a tell-tale sign. You might find yourself feeling stuck, unmotivated, or even questioning if all the effort is worth it. Unfortunately, this is not abnormal and is just part of the process. Plateaus can be frustrating, but they are not a failure. They are simply a pause, a moment to catch your breath and reassess.

If you find yourself in this position, consider whether your routine has become too rigid or predictable. One strategy to break through these plateaus is to try new somatic techniques. Sometimes, your body and mind become too accustomed to a routine, and introducing a new practice can reignite progress. If you've been focusing on breathwork, try incorporating more movement-based exercises like dance or gentle yoga. If grounding exercises have been your go-to, experiment with visualization techniques. The novelty of a new practice can stimulate your mind and body, helping you move past the stagnation. Additionally, allowing yourself the freedom to skip a practice every now and then can provide a much-needed refresh, making it easier to return with renewed energy. Seeking professional guidance can also be immensely beneficial. A trained somatic therapist or other can offer fresh perspectives and specialized techniques to help you overcome obstacles. They can help you identify areas that need more focus and provide the support necessary to manage through the plateau.

When overcoming plateaus, a supportive somatic community offers emotional and social support, shared experiences, and learning opportunities. Join new groups or classes where you can connect with others who share your interests. Search for local meetups focused on somatic practices or trauma recovery. Online forums can be a treasure trove of experiences, tips, and support. Sharing your challenges and progress with others can provide a sense of accountability and motivation. It's like having a team cheering you on, celebrating your victories, and lifting you up when you stumble.

Revisiting your goals and practices is another effective strategy. As you progress, your needs and priorities may shift. Take some time to reassess your goals to ensure they align with your current state. Adjusting goals based on your current needs can provide a renewed sense of purpose and direction. If a goal feels too ambitious, break it down into smaller, more manageable steps. Modifying your practices can also help renew your engagement. If a particular exercise feels stale or ineffective, don't hesitate to tweak it or try something different. Remember to keep your practices dynamic and responsive to your evolving needs.

Consider joining somatic yoga or movement classes. These classes offer structured guidance and the opportunity to practice in a group setting. The collective energy of a class can be incredibly motivating. Participating in community workshops, whether in person or online, can also provide fresh perspectives and techniques. These workshops often introduce new practices and offer a sense of camaraderie. Online somatic communities are another valuable resource. They provide a platform to share your journey, ask questions, and receive support from a broad network of people. Being part of an online community means you can access support anytime, anywhere.

. . .

Support groups are another resource for guidance and encouragement, offering connections with others who can provide new perspectives and motivation. Whether it's an in-person group or an online community, the shared experiences and collective knowledge can be incredibly uplifting. You'll find that others have faced similar challenges and can offer practical advice and emotional support. Sometimes, knowing you're not alone in your struggles can make a world of difference.

Accountability partnerships can also be a great option. Find someone, maybe in a support group, who is also committed to their healing journey and agrees to check in with each other regularly. Share your goals, challenges, and progress. Knowing that someone else is holding you accountable can provide the extra push you need to stay on track. Attend retreats if possible. These immersive experiences can offer a profound reset and a deeper dive into somatic practices. Being in a different environment, focusing solely on your healing, can provide eye-opening revelations and breakthroughs.

Lastly, remember to practice self-compassion and give yourself grace during these times. It's easy to be hard on yourself when progress slows, but this only adds to the burden. Treat yourself with the same care and consideration you would offer a friend. Remember, it's okay to take a step back and evaluate where you are. Acknowledge the effort you're putting in, even if the results aren't immediate.

Incorporating these strategies can help you overcome plateaus and setbacks, keeping your whole experience varied and responsive to your needs. By trying new techniques, seeking support, revisiting goals, and engaging with a supportive community, you can move through the challenges and continue to grow.

CONNECTING WITH YOUR TRUE SELF

Somatic pathways offer a powerful means of self-discovery and connecting with your true self. At times, this can feel like trying to tune into a distant radio station—static, interference, and snippets of clarity. It's all about leaning into authenticity and self-awareness. Think of it as stripping away the layers of societal expectations, past traumas, and self-doubt that no longer serve you to reveal the core of who you are. It's that inner voice that knows what you need, even if you've spent years ignoring it. Connecting with this part of yourself is imperative to your personal growth because it allows you to live in alignment with your true values and desires, even if they go against the grain. As Brené Brown, a prominent researcher of shame and empathy, wisely states, "True belonging doesn't require you to change who you are; it requires you to be who you are." It's about being true to yourself, even when it's uncomfortable or challenging. This level of authenticity creates a sense of freedom and empowerment, allowing you to live a life that genuinely reflects who you are. It might mean pursuing a career that fulfills you, building relationships that nurture you, or engaging in activities that bring you joy. It's like finally finding that clear frequency where your favorite song plays uninterrupted.

Your inner wisdom is always there, patiently waiting for you to tune in and listen. We often get caught up in what we think we should do rather than what feels right. This disconnect can lead to a sense of unease or fragmentation. By tuning into how you feel instead of what you think, you begin to bridge this gap. Imagine navigating through life using a compass that always points true north. It guides you towards what truly speaks to you, helping you make decisions that are in line with your authentic self. It's about trusting your gut, even when your mind is clouded with doubt. Embracing authenticity is a natural outcome of somatic healing.

. . .

Trauma often leaves us with an overly judgmental inner voice that criticizes and berates us for our perceived shortcomings. Making choices based on somatic insights keeps you from getting lost in your head. You learn to feel your way through situations. Somatic healing prompts you to treat yourself with warmth and acceptance. By tuning into your body's signals, you learn to respond with empathy rather than criticism. This creates a nurturing environment for healing, allowing you to release old patterns and embrace new possibilities to create a life that feels meaningful and fulfilling.

As you continue to explore these somatic methods, remember that connecting with your true self is a "journey, not a destination." There will be moments of clarity and moments of confusion, but each step brings you closer to yourself. Embrace the process with curiosity and know that you are uncovering the authentic core of who you are.

CONCLUSION

Reading this book is a big step towards healing. Remember, the primary goal here is to give you practical tools to heal and cope with your trauma through somatic therapy. The techniques we've covered are not quick fixes, but with consistent practice, they can profoundly enhance your mind-body connection, so you can trust your inner guide and build emotional resilience, and overall well-being.

Let's take a moment to recap all that we have covered together. We started with the basics of somatic therapy, diving into what it is and how it can help you heal. Next, we detailed the profound impact trauma has on both your body and mind, laying the groundwork for why somatic therapy is so effective. We then delved into the science behind somatic healing, unraveling the complexities of your nervous system and how it can be regulated for better emotional clarity. The core techniques chapter was packed with actionable practices— grounding exercises, breathwork, gentle movement, progressive muscle relaxation, somatic resourcing and more. Highlighting how these practices enable you to release stored tension and emotional pain. Additionally, they help restore a sense of safety and regulation within your nervous system, leading to significant symptom relief, including reduced anxiety, improved emotional regulation, and better sleep. Moreover, each technique is designed to be practical and easy to integrate into your daily life. We also discussed how to tailor these practices to address specific types of trauma, whether it's childhood trauma, PTSD, complex trauma, physical trauma, sexual trauma, or relationship trauma. This personalized approach ensures that you can find the techniques that align best with your unique experiences.

Then, we talked about integrating somatic therapy with other healing modalities, like talk therapy CBT and EMDR, to create a more comprehensive approach to healing. We even touched upon how technology can enhance your somatic practices, offering tools and apps for extra support. From there, we discussed the very important topic of how to apply them in real life and create your very own personal practice. Then, for extra measure, we covered how to ensure your continued healing, personal growth, and success.

The first key takeaway is that healing is not linear- this path has twists, turns, bumps, and occasional detours. Be patient with yourself and celebrate every small victory along the way. Second, your body holds incredible wisdom. By tuning into your physical sensations, you can unlock a wealth of knowledge that guides you not only toward healing but also heightens your intuition and alignment with your true self. Third, consistency is king. Small, regular practices can accumulate over time, leading to remarkable changes in your emotional and physical health.

If you're looking for more resources, there are plenty of avenues to explore. I have included a Somatic Therapy Resources section at the end of this book with a variety of extra material like guided audio, progress tracking, reflections, somatic practice planning and more along with additional information to look into further. Also, if you are interested in learning more about somatic therapy, online and in-person workshops, and programs can offer deeper dives into these practices. You also may want to consider finding a practitioner or facilitator who can guide you through more personalized sessions.

Now, it's time for action! Start by applying the techniques we've discussed, remembering that you hold the power to transform your life through somatic therapy. Gaining control over your state of being is life changing. It might take some practice, and yes, you may stumble occasionally, but that's all part of the process. The more you work on it, the easier it becomes, and the slip-ups happen less often. As you continue to practice, you'll build confidence and learn to trust yourself. You'll also learn to really like and even love the person you are, opening the door to deeper connections with yourself and others. I have complete confidence in your ability to achieve a renewed sense of self and strengthen your emotional resilience. With the resources and tools you've gained from this book, you're well-equipped to overcome trauma and lead a fulfilling life.

Lastly, I want to express my gratitude. Thank you for taking the time to engage with this book and for your commitment to healing. Your courage and effort in taking this step is commendable!

CONTINUING THE JOURNEY OF TRANSFORMATION

YOUR OPINION MATTERS!

Now you have the powerful tools you need to release emotional pain and cultivate a deeper mind-body connection. It's time to share your newfound knowledge and guide other readers to the same support.

By leaving your honest opinion of this book on Amazon, you'll help others interested in somatic therapy for trauma find the information they're searching for and inspire them to take their first steps toward healing.

Thank you for your support! 🩶 The path to healing continues when we share our insights—and you're playing a vital role in that process.

Scan to Review

SOMATIC THERAPY RESOURCES

GUIDED EXERCISE AUDIO RECORDINGS

Scan for Bonus
Guided Audio

BONUS WORKSHEETS

Use the tracking worksheets and journal prompts to make it even easier to track your progress and gain insights to tailor your practice to ensure your accountability to yourself for your growth and healing.

Scan for Bonus
Worksheets

APPS TO SUPPORT YOUR SOMATIC THERAPY PRACTICE:

- **SomaShare**: [SomaShare Website](https://somashare.com) (available on app stores)
- **Embodymind**: https://apps.apple.com/us/app/embodymind/id6477547367 / https://play.google.com/store/apps/details?id=com.arketa.embodymind&hl=en_US
- **NEUROFIT**: [NEUROFIT Website](https://neurofit.app) (available on app stores)
- **Somawell**: https://apps.apple.com/ca/app/somawell/id6526468592
- **SomaIQ**: https://apps.apple.com/us/app/soma-iq/id6476015454 / https://play.google.com/store/apps/details?id=com.kj2147491990.app&hl=en_US (available on app stores)
- **Breathe2Relax**: https://apps.apple.com/us/app/breathe2relax/id425720246 / https://play.google.com/

store/apps/details?id=mil.dha.breathe2relax&hl=en_US /
(available on app stores)

- **Othership**: [OthershipWebsite] (https://www.othership.
  us/app) (available on app stores)
- **Insight Timer**: [Insight Timer Website](https://
  insighttimer.com)
- **Headspace**: [Headspace Website](https://www.
  headspace.com)
- **Calm**: [Calm Website](https://www.calm.com)
- **Smiling Mind**: [Smiling Mind Website](https://
  smilingmind.com.au)
- **Day One:** https://dayoneapp.com (available on app stores)
  – A journaling app designed to help you document your
  thoughts and experiences, promoting self-reflection and
  emotional processing.

*Please verify the availability of each app and tech device, as they
may have updated or changed over time.

WEARABLE DEVICES TO SUPPORT SOMATIC PRACTICE:

- Apple Watch
  - Welltory app- Advanced HRV tracking
- Oura Ring- https://ouraring.com/

VIRTUAL REALITY APPS:

- **TRIPP**: https://www.tripp.com
- **Guided Meditation VR**: https://
  Guidedmeditationvr.com/
- **Nature Treks VR**: Meta Quest: https://www.meta.com/
  experiences/nature-treks-vr/2616537008386430/ Steam:

https://store.steampowered.com/app/587580/
Nature_Treks_VR/

YOUTUBE SEARCH TERMS FOR GUIDED SOMATIC PRACTICES:

- Guided grounding techniques
- Guided somatic resourcing
- Guided somatic visualization
- Guided Progressive Muscle Relaxation
- Guided somatic movement
- Guided Somatic dance
- Guided Mindful touch
- Somatic self-massage
- Somatic breathing techniques for trauma, anxiety, or stress relief
- Titration or pendulation to release trauma
- Guided somatic practice
- Guided Titration
- Guided Pendulation
- Guided somatic visualizations
- Guided somatic exercises
- Guided somatic breathwork
- Guided somatic tracking Guided somatic sleep meditation Guided somatic release
- Guided somatic yoga Guided soma breathwork
- Guided somatic therapy
- Guided somatic
- Guided somatic body scan
- Guided somatic tracking

*This is not an exhaustive list

LEADERS IN SOMATIC THERAPY

- **Peter Levine**: Creator of Somatic Experiencing™, a body-oriented approach to trauma healing that emphasizes the role of the body in processing traumatic experiences.
- **Bessel van der Kolk**: Author of *The Body Keeps the Score*, known for his extensive research on trauma and its effects on the body, advocating for integrative treatments that include somatic practices.
- **Pat Ogden**: Founder of the Sensorimotor Psychotherapy Institute, known for combining somatic therapy with cognitive approaches to address trauma and attachment issues.
- **Gabor Maté**: Renowned for his work on addiction, stress, and childhood trauma, he emphasizes the importance of body awareness in healing emotional and psychological wounds.
- **Stephen Porges**: Developer of the Polyvagal Theory, which explores how our physiological state influences behavior and emotions, particularly in relation to trauma and social connection.
- **Tara Brach**: Psychologist and meditation teacher known for integrating mindfulness and somatic awareness in her therapeutic work, focusing on self-compassion and healing.
- **Resmaa Menakem**: A therapist and author known for his work on racialized trauma, emphasizing the importance of somatic practices in addressing collective trauma.
- **Ruth Lanius**: A leading researcher in the field of trauma and its effects on the brain, advocating for somatic and neurobiological approaches to therapy.

ADVANCED APPROACHES & METHODS FOR FURTHER EXPLORATION

- **Sensorimotor Psychotherapy**: Created by Pat Ogden, this approach integrates cognitive and somatic techniques to help clients process trauma and develop body awareness.
- **Tension and Trauma Releasing Exercises (TRE®)**: Developed by David Berceli, TRE involves a series of exercises designed to release deep muscular patterns of stress, tension, and trauma through tremoring.
- **Somatic Experiencing® (SE™)**: Developed by Peter Levine, SE focuses on the body's natural ability to heal from trauma by addressing physiological responses and releasing stored tension.
- **Body-Mind Centering (BMC®)**: Founded by Bonnie Bainbridge Cohen, BMC explores the relationship between movement, body awareness, and consciousness, integrating somatic practices into various therapeutic settings.
- **Hakomi Method®**: Founded by Ron Kurtz and a group of trainers, this body-centered psychotherapy emphasizes mindfulness and the exploration of core beliefs through somatic awareness, promoting deep self-discovery.
- **Trauma Resiliency Model (TRM®)**: This model focuses on building resilience through an understanding of trauma's effects and integrating somatic strategies to support recovery and well-being.
- **Focusing**: Created by Eugene Gendlin, this technique guides clients to pay attention to bodily sensations to facilitate emotional awareness and healing.

REFERENCES

Online Articles and Publications

Harvard Health Publishing. (2023, July 7). *What is somatic therapy?* https://www.health.harvard.edu/blog/what-is-somatic-therapy-202307072951

Elkind, J. (2023, March 16). *Somatic therapy: Benefits, types, and efficacy.* Forbes. https://www.forbes.com/health/mind/somatic-therapy/

ICANotes. (2024, March 28). *Somatic experiencing for trauma recovery.* https://www.icanotes.com/2024/03/28/somatic-experiencing-therapy-for-trauma-recovery/#:~:text=Body%20awareness%20plays%20a%20critical,responds%20to%20triggers%20and%20stress.

FirstSession. (n.d.). *Somatic therapy exercises and techniques.* https://www.firstsession.com/resources/somatic-therapy-exercises-techniques

National Center for Biotechnology Information. (n.d.). *Understanding the impact of trauma.* https://www.ncbi.nlm.nih.gov/books/NBK207191/#:~:text=Initial%20reactions%20to%20trauma%20can,effective%2C%20and%20self%2Dlimited.

National Child Traumatic Stress Network. (n.d.). *Trauma types.* https://www.nctsn.org/what-is-child-trauma/trauma-types

National Center for Biotechnology Information. (n.d.). *Understanding the impact of trauma.* https://www.ncbi.nlm.nih.gov/books/NBK207191/#:~:text=Delayed%20responses%20to%20trauma%20can,1%20outlines%20some%20common%20reactions.

NICABM. (n.d.). *Polyvagal theory and how trauma impacts the body.* https://www.nicabm.com/trauma-polyvagal-theory-and-how-trauma-impacts-the-body/

Kiser, L. J. (2011). *Traumatic stress: Effects on the brain.* PMC. https://www.ncbi.nlm.nih.gov/pmc/articles/PMC3181836/

Quantum University. (n.d.). *Neuroplasticity.* https://quantumuniversity.com/courses/neuroplasticity/

Kessler, R. C., & Wang, P. S. (2010). *Post-traumatic stress disorder: The neurobiological impact.* PMC. https://www.ncbi.nlm.nih.gov/pmc/articles/PMC3182008/

Schubert, C. (2021). *Somatic experiencing – Effectiveness and key factors of a therapeutic approach.* PMC. https://www.ncbi.nlm.nih.gov/pmc/articles/PMC8276649/

Healthline. (2022, April 25). *30 grounding techniques to quiet distressing thoughts.* https://www.healthline.com/health/grounding-techniques

Ergos Institute. (n.d.). *Peter A. Levine, PhD.* https://www.somaticexperiencing.com/about-peter

Sood, A. (2021). *Effectiveness of progressive muscle relaxation, deep breathing, and guided imagery in reducing anxiety.* PMC. https://www.ncbi.nlm.nih.gov/pmc/articles/PMC8272667/

Somatic Therapy Partners. (n.d.). *The complete guide for using somatic therapy for trauma.* https://somatictherapypartners.com/somatic-therapy-for-trauma-healing-guide/

Pyramid Healthcare. (n.d.). *Treating trauma with polyvagal theory.* https://www.pyramid-healthcare.com/treating-trauma-with-polyvagal-theory/#:~:text=Somatic%20therapy%20is%20a%20body,or%20trapped%20in%20the%20body.

TalkHealthRive. (n.d.). *Unveiling the power of somatic therapy.* https://talkhealthrive.com/post/unveiling-the-power-of-somatic-therapy-a-pathway-to-healing-from-within/

Bay Area CBT Center. (n.d.). *Somatic experiencing in CBT: Enhancing trauma treatment.* https://bayareacbtcenter.com/the-role-of-somatic-experiencing-in-cbt/

LaCaze, E. (n.d.). *Combining somatic experiencing and EMDR for trauma therapy.* https://www.elizabethlacaze.com/blog/combining-somatic-experiencing-and-emdr-for-trauma-therapy

Neurofit. (n.d.). *NEUROFIT app | Nervous system reset | Somatic exercises.* https://neurofit.app/

Valluri, S. (2022). *NURSE: Five micro-practices to reduce stress.* Watson Caring Science. https://www.watsoncaringscience.org/files/PDF/Articles/NURSE%20-Valluri%202022.pdf

ScienceDirect. (n.d.). *Somatic marker hypothesis - an overview.* https://www.sciencedirect.com/topics/neuroscience/somatic-marker-hypothesis#:~:text=The%20somatic%20marker%20hypothesis%20is%20one%20of%20the%20most%20influential,afferent%20feedback%20to%20the%20brain.

Autonomous.ai. (n.d.). *Somatic therapy: Restoring mind-body dynamics at work.* https://www.autonomous.ai/ourblog/somatic-therapy-in-the-office-environment

Repose. (n.d.). *Somatic therapy techniques to combat insomnia: A holistic approach.* https://byrepose.com/journal/somatic-therapy-techniques-to-combat-insomnia

MyWellbeing. (n.d.). *Understanding somatic therapy and its benefits.* https://mywellbeing.com/therapy-101/exploring-the-depths-of-somatic-therapy#:~:text=The%20therapist%20attentively%20tracks%20the,support%20their%20self%2Dexploration%20process.

Talkspace. (n.d.). *So, you've hit a plateau in therapy — now what?* https://www.talkspace.com/blog/therapy-progress-stuck/

Life by Design Therapy. (2023, June 1). *The body-mind connection: A guide to somatic therapy and its techniques.* https://www.lifebydesigntherapy.com/blog/the-body-mind-connection-a-guide-to-somatic-therapy-and-its-techniques/6/2023#:~:text=Body%2DMind%20Connection%3A%20As%20already,understanding%20of%20their%20present%20experiences.

Books

Clear, J. (2018). *Atomic habits: An easy & proven way to build good habits & break bad ones.* Avery.

Dispenza, J. (2012). *Breaking the habit of being yourself: How to lose your mind and create a new one.* Hay House.

Mate, G. (2003). *When the body says no: Exploring the stress-disease connection.* Wiley.

Brown, K. W., Ryan, R. M., & Creswell, J. D. (2012). Mindfulness interventions. *Annual Review of Psychology, 63,* 601-626. https://doi.org/10.1146/annurev-psych-120710-100031

Creswell, J. D., Way, B. R., Eisenberger, N. I., & Lieberman, M. D. (2016). Neuroimaging of social rejection: Effects of a mindfulness intervention. *Psychological Science, 27*(1), 58-68. https://doi.org/10.1177/0956797615613863

Levine, P. (2010). *In an unspoken voice: How the body releases trauma and restores goodness.* North Atlantic Books.

Ogden, P., Minton, K., & Pain, C. (2006). *Sensorimotor psychotherapy: Interventions for trauma and attachment.* Norton & Company.

Van der Kolk, B. A. (2007). *The body keeps the score: Brain, mind, and body in the healing of trauma.* Viking.

Van der Kolk, B. A. (2014). The body keeps the score: Mind, brain, and body in the healing of trauma. *Psychological Trauma: Theory, Research, Practice, and Policy, 6*(5), 518-523. https://doi.org/10.1037/tra0000030

Case Studies

Levine, P. A. (2010). In an unspoken voice: How the body releases trauma and restores goodness. This book discusses various case studies and the impact of somatic therapies on childhood trauma.

Ogden, P., Minton, K., & Pain, C. (2006). Trauma and the body: A sensorimotor approach to psychotherapy. This work includes accounts of veterans using somatic therapy techniques such as breathwork to address PTSD symptoms.

Heller, L., & Heller, A. (2013). *Healing developmental trauma: How to acknowledge, understand, and treat childhood trauma.* This book covers concepts of safe touch and somatic practices aimed at rebuilding.

www.ingramcontent.com/pod-product-compliance
Ingram Content Group UK Ltd.
Pitfield, Milton Keynes, MK11 3LW, UK
UKHW020811220525
6039UKWH00018B/202